MAJOR WORLD LEADERS

YASIR ARAFAT

MENACHEM BEGIN

TONY BLAIR

GEORGE W. BUSH

JIMMY CARTER

FIDEL CASTRO

VICENTE FOX

SADDAM HUSSEIN

HAMID KARZAI

KIM IL SUNG AND KIM JONG IL

HOSNI MUBARAK

PERVEZ MUSHARRAF

VLADIMIR PUTIN

MOHAMMED REZA PAHLAVI

ANWAR SADAT

THE SAUDI ROYAL FAMILY

GERHARD SCHROEDER

ARIEL SHARON

Ariel Sharon

Richard Worth

CHELSEA HOUSE
PUBLISHERS
A Haights Cross Communications Company
Philadelphia

Frontis: Sharon at Western Wall

CHELSEA HOUSE PUBLISHERS

V.P., New Product Development Sally Cheney
Director of Production Kim Shinners
Creative Manager Takeshi Takahashi
Manufacturing Manager Diann Grasse

Staff for ARIEL SHARON

Executive Editor Lee Marcott
Senior Editor Tara Koellhoffer
Production Assistant Megan Emery
Picture Research 21st Century Publishing and Communications, Inc.
Series and Cover Designer Takeshi Takahashi
Layout 21st Century Publishing and Communications, Inc.

A Haights Cross Communications ✦ Company

http://www.chelseahouse.com

First Printing

1 3 5 7 9 8 6 4 2

Library of Congress Cataloging-in-Publication Data

Worth, Richard.
   Ariel Sharon / Richard Worth.
      p. cm.—(Major world leaders)
Summary: A biography of Ariel Sharon, the man who was re-elected Prime Minister of
Israel in January 2003. Includes bibliographical references and index.
   ISBN 0-7910-7653-9 (Hardcover)
   1. Sharon, Ariel—Juvenile literature. 2. Prime ministers—Israel—Biography—Juvenile
literature. 3. Generals—Israel—Biography—Juvenile literature. 4. Israel—Politics and
government—20th century—Juvenile literature. 5. Israel—Biography—Juvenile literature.
[1. Sharon, Ariel. 2. Prime ministers. 3. Jews—Biography.] I. Title. II. Series.
DS126.6.S42W67 2003
956.9405'4'092—dc21

                                                                            2003009500

TABLE OF CONTENTS

Foreword: On Leadership
Arthur M. Schlesinger, jr.   6

1   Victory   12

2   Creating the State of Israel   26

3   War After War   40

4   Sharon, the Politician   54

5   Battling the Palestinians   66

6   The Quest for Peace   76

7   Prime Minister   88

    Chronology   94
    Bibliography   95
    Index   96

On Leadership

Arthur M. Schlesinger, jr.

Leadership, it may be said, is really what makes the world go round. Love no doubt smoothes the passage; but love is a private transaction between consenting adults. Leadership is a public transaction with history. The idea of leadership affirms the capacity of individuals to move, inspire, and mobilize masses of people so that they act together in pursuit of an end. Sometimes leadership serves good purposes, sometimes bad; but whether the end is benign or evil, great leaders are those men and women who leave their personal stamp on history.

Now, the very concept of leadership implies the proposition that individuals can make a difference. This proposition has never been universally accepted. From classical times to the present day, eminent thinkers have regarded individuals as no more than the agents and pawns of larger forces, whether the gods and goddesses of the ancient world or, in the modern era, race, class, nation, the dialectic, the will of the people, the spirit of the times, history itself. Against such forces, the individual dwindles into insignificance.

So contends the thesis of historical determinism. Tolstoy's great novel *War and Peace* offers a famous statement of the case. Why, Tolstoy asked, did millions of men in the Napoleonic Wars, denying their human feelings and their common sense, move back and forth across Europe slaughtering their fellows? "The war," Tolstoy answered, "was bound to happen simply because it was bound to happen." All prior history determined it. As for leaders, they, Tolstoy said, "are but the labels that serve to give a name to an end and, like labels, they have the least possible connection with the event." The greater the leader, "the more conspicuous the inevitability and the predestination of every act he commits." The leader, said Tolstoy, is "the slave of history."

Determinism takes many forms. Marxism is the determinism of class. Nazism the determinism of race. But the idea of men and women as the slaves of history runs athwart the deepest human instincts. Rigid determinism abolishes the idea of human freedom—the assumption of free choice that underlies every move we make, every word we speak, every thought we think. It abolishes the idea of human responsibility,

since it is manifestly unfair to reward or punish people for actions that are by definition beyond their control. No one can live consistently by any deterministic creed. The Marxist states prove this themselves by their extreme susceptibility to the cult of leadership.

More than that, history refutes the idea that individuals make no difference. In December 1931 a British politician crossing Fifth Avenue in New York City between 76th and 77th Streets around 10:30 P.M. looked in the wrong direction and was knocked down by an automobile—a moment, he later recalled, of a man aghast, a world aglare: "I do not understand why I was not broken like an eggshell or squashed like a gooseberry." Fourteen months later an American politician, sitting in an open car in Miami, Florida, was fired on by an assassin; the man beside him was hit. Those who believe that individuals make no difference to history might well ponder whether the next two decades would have been the same had Mario Constasino's car killed Winston Churchill in 1931 and Giuseppe Zangara's bullet killed Franklin Roosevelt in 1933. Suppose, in addition, that Lenin had died of typhus in Siberia in 1895 and that Hitler had been killed on the Western Front in 1916. What would the 20th century have looked like now?

For better or for worse, individuals do make a difference. "The notion that a people can run itself and its affairs anonymously," wrote the philosopher William James, "is now well known to be the silliest of absurdities. Mankind does nothing save through initiatives on the part of inventors, great or small, and imitation by the rest of us—these are the sole factors in human progress. Individuals of genius show the way, and set the patterns, which common people then adopt and follow."

Leadership, James suggests, means leadership in thought as well as in action. In the long run, leaders in thought may well make the greater difference to the world. "The ideas of economists and political philosophers, both when they are right and when they are wrong," wrote John Maynard Keynes, "are more powerful than is commonly understood. Indeed the world is ruled by little else. Practical men, who believe themselves to be quite exempt from any intellectual influences, are usually the slaves of some defunct economist. . . . The power of vested interests is vastly exaggerated compared with the gradual encroachment of ideas."

But, as Woodrow Wilson once said, "Those only are leaders of men, in the general eye, who lead in action. . . . It is at their hands that new thought gets its translation into the crude language of deeds." Leaders in thought often invent in solitude and obscurity, leaving to later generations the tasks of imitation. Leaders in action—the leaders portrayed in this series—have to be effective in their own time.

And they cannot be effective by themselves. They must act in response to the rhythms of their age. Their genius must be adapted, in a phrase from William James, "to the receptivities of the moment." Leaders are useless without followers. "There goes the mob," said the French politician, hearing a clamor in the streets. "I am their leader. I must follow them." Great leaders turn the inchoate emotions of the mob to purposes of their own. They seize on the opportunities of their time, the hopes, fears, frustrations, crises, potentialities. They succeed when events have prepared the way for them, when the community is awaiting to be aroused, when they can provide the clarifying and organizing ideas. Leadership completes the circuit between the individual and the mass and thereby alters history.

It may alter history for better or for worse. Leaders have been responsible for the most extravagant follies and most monstrous crimes that have beset suffering humanity. They have also been vital in such gains as humanity has made in individual freedom, religious and racial tolerance, social justice, and respect for human rights.

There is no sure way to tell in advance who is going to lead for good and who for evil. But a glance at the gallery of men and women in MAJOR WORLD LEADERS suggests some useful tests.

One test is this: Do leaders lead by force or by persuasion? By command or by consent? Through most of history leadership was exercised by the divine right of authority. The duty of followers was to defer and to obey. "Theirs not to reason why/Theirs but to do and die." On occasion, as with the so-called enlightened despots of the 18th century in Europe, absolutist leadership was animated by humane purposes. More often, absolutism nourished the passion for domination, land, gold, and conquest and resulted in tyranny.

The great revolution of modern times has been the revolution of equality. "Perhaps no form of government," wrote the British historian James Bryce in his study of the United States, *The American Commonwealth*, "needs great leaders so much as democracy." The idea that all people should be equal in their legal condition has undermined the old structure of authority, hierarchy, and deference. The revolution of equality has had two contrary effects on the nature of leadership. For equality, as Alexis de Tocqueville pointed out in his great study *Democracy in America*, might mean equality in servitude as well as equality in freedom.

"I know of only two methods of establishing equality in the political world," Tocqueville wrote. "Rights must be given to every citizen, or none at all to anyone . . . save one, who is the master of all." There was no middle ground "between the sovereignty of all and the absolute power of one man." In his astonishing prediction of 20th-century totalitarian dictatorship, Tocqueville explained how the revolution of equality could lead to the *Führerprinzip* and more terrible absolutism than the world had ever known.

But when rights are given to every citizen and the sovereignty of all is established, the problem of leadership takes a new form, becomes more exacting than ever before. It is easy to issue commands and enforce them by the rope and the stake, the concentration camp and the *gulag*. It is much harder to use argument and achievement to overcome opposition and win consent. The Founding Fathers of the United States understood the difficulty. They believed that history had given them the opportunity to decide, as Alexander Hamilton wrote in the first Federalist Paper, whether men are indeed capable of basing government on "reflection and choice, or whether they are forever destined to depend . . . on accident and force."

Government by reflection and choice called for a new style of leadership and a new quality of followership. It required leaders to be responsive to popular concerns, and it required followers to be active and informed participants in the process. Democracy does not eliminate emotion from politics; sometimes it fosters demagoguery; but it is confident that, as the greatest of democratic leaders put it, you cannot fool all of the people all of the time. It measures leadership by results and retires those who overreach or falter or fail.

It is true that in the long run despots are measured by results too. But they can postpone the day of judgment, sometimes indefinitely, and in the meantime they can do infinite harm. It is also true that democracy is no guarantee of virtue and intelligence in government, for the voice of the people is not necessarily the voice of God. But democracy, by assuring the right of opposition, offers built-in resistance to the evils inherent in absolutism. As the theologian Reinhold Niebuhr summed it up, "Man's capacity for justice makes democracy possible, but man's inclination to justice makes democracy necessary."

A second test for leadership is the end for which power is sought. When leaders have as their goal the supremacy of a master race or the promotion of totalitarian revolution or the acquisition and exploitation of colonies or the protection of greed and privilege or the preservation of personal power, it is likely that their leadership will do little to advance the cause of humanity. When their goal is the abolition of slavery, the liberation of women, the enlargement of opportunity for the poor and powerless, the extension of equal rights to racial minorities, the defense of the freedoms of expression and opposition, it is likely that their leadership will increase the sum of human liberty and welfare.

Leaders have done great harm to the world. They have also conferred great benefits. You will find both sorts in this series. Even "good" leaders must be regarded with a certain wariness. Leaders are not demigods; they put on their trousers one leg after another just like ordinary mortals. No leader is infallible, and every leader needs to be reminded of this at regular intervals. Irreverence irritates leaders but is their salvation. Unquestioning submission corrupts leaders and demeans followers. Making a cult of a leader is always a mistake. Fortunately hero worship generates its own antidote. "Every hero," said Emerson, "becomes a bore at last."

The signal benefit the great leaders confer is to embolden the rest of us to live according to our own best selves, to be active, insistent, and resolute in affirming our own sense of things. For great leaders attest to the reality of human freedom against the supposed inevitabilities of history. And they attest to the wisdom and power that may lie within the most unlikely of us, which is why Abraham Lincoln remains the supreme example of great leadership. A great leader, said Emerson, exhibits new possibilities to all humanity. "We feed on genius. . . . Great men exist that there may be greater men."

Great leaders, in short, justify themselves by emancipating and empowering their followers. So humanity struggles to master its destiny, remembering with Alexis de Tocqueville: "It is true that around every man a fatal circle is traced beyond which he cannot pass; but within the wide verge of that circle he is powerful and free; as it is with man, so with communities." ■

Victory

"**H**istoric," Ariel Sharon called it. He was referring to his re-election as prime minister of Israel in late January 2003. "Arik [Sharon's nickname]—king of Israel," his supporters shouted during a rally after the election. It was one of the greatest victories in the history of the Likud Party and an enormous personal triumph for the prime minister himself. Sharon had helped found *Likud*, which means "unity," in 1973. Since then he had held various positions in Likud governments, including defense minister and foreign minister. He was finally elected prime minister for the first time in 2001.

His re-election was even more impressive and showed that many Israelis supported his leadership. As a result of the 2003 election, Likud won 40 seats in the Israeli parliament, called the Knesset. Sharon needed a majority of 61 seats in the 120-seat parliament to

Ariel Sharon waved to supporters after being reelected prime minister of Israel on January 28, 2003.

govern Israel—one party normally does not win a majority. Therefore, he joined with several other small political parties to form a coalition government.

Sharon's victory came amid charges of corruption in the Likud Party. The prime minister was being investigated for illegal contributions to his 1999 campaign for Likud leadership. According to investigators, Likud had accepted a $1.5 million contribution from an American company, Annex Research. Financial assistance from a foreign company during an election campaign is illegal in Israel. Sharon contended that he knew nothing about the contribution. He also argued that he was unaware that the money was paid back by a South African businessman named Cyril Kern, who was a close friend of Sharon's.

Sharon was extremely angry about these accusations of wrongdoing. During the election campaign, he went on television and loudly began to criticize the opposition parties for creating the scandal. He was especially critical of his main opponent, Amram Mitzna, the leader of the Labor Party, the main rival of Likud in the election. Sharon began pounding the podium as he was speaking. He accused Mitzna of trying to win the election and "seize power through lies."

Under Israeli law, a candidate is not allowed to make political speeches and use propaganda on television during a campaign. The television stations were ordered to immediately end the broadcast. Suddenly television screens went blank in millions of homes in Israel. As this happened, the prime minister's words were still being heard: "Have you gone crazy?" he said. "Have you gone mad? People tell lies, they tell lies, all kinds of gossip."

Before the broadcast, Likud had been losing ground in the election. Many voters seemed to believe the reports of corruption. Some of the Likud candidates running for seats in the Knesset were also being investigated. News reports said that they might have paid off crime figures who then arranged for them to be nominated to run in the election. Polls in early January showed that Sharon's popularity and the position of Likud were declining. But the television incident seemed to change everything. As one voter said, "I'd decided not to vote at all. But, after what they did to Sharon, I'm going back to the Likud. In what country do they treat a prime minister like this?"

Many voters were outraged that a prime minister could be taken off the air. They began to rally to Sharon. One reason was the tough position he had taken over the previous two years against the Palestinians. Sharon was in a long-running battle with the Palestinian leader Yasir Arafat over the future of a Palestinian state. The Palestinian Authority, which was led by Chairman Arafat, governed territories in the Gaza Strip along the Mediterranean coast and on the West Bank of the Jordan River. Arafat and the Palestinians believed they were entitled to more territory on the West Bank. Sharon disagreed, wanting to limit Palestinian settlements to about 40 percent of the West Bank territory. Sharon claimed the rest for Israel. Meanwhile, the prime minister was expanding Israeli settlements on the West Bank.

The Palestinians were outraged by what the Israelis were doing. Since the Israeli army was much stronger than the forces of the Palestinian Authority, there seemed to be no way to stop the Jews. Some Palestinians volunteered to sacrifice themselves as suicide bombers. They were prepared to end their own lives for the Palestinian cause and kill Israeli citizens. By bringing violence inside Israel, they hoped to persuade the Sharon government to grant the Palestinians more land.

Many of these bombers are young men and women, often teenagers. According to one expert, they are extremely angry and feel humiliated because Israel occupies territory that Palestinians believe rightfully belongs to them. "Shame is the most painful emotion in the Arab culture," this expert said, "producing the feeling that one is unworthy to live. The honorable Arab is the one who refuses to suffer shame and dies in dignity."

Suicide bombings had occurred in the past. But during

In the years since Sharon's election, violence has plagued the streets of Israel. Here, Israeli police treat victims of a suicide attack that killed at least 19 people in Jerusalem in August 2001.

the two years since Sharon's first election in 2001, the number of bombings rose to a level never before seen in Israel. The suicide bombers came into Israel with hidden bombs strapped to their bodies. They selected populated locations in Israeli cities and set off the bombs. The bombers themselves were killed, along with many innocent Israeli civilians. In

January 2003, for example, two suicide bombers blew themselves up in Tel Aviv. Twenty-two Israelis were killed and more than 100 were wounded.

Meanwhile, during the same period, clashes occurred between the Israeli army and other Palestinian terrorists. Palestinian gunmen entered an Israeli town near the West Bank and murdered a resident. In retaliation, Israeli soldiers hunted down the gunmen and killed them. An Israeli helicopter also launched missiles at a car in Gaza thought to be carrying a Palestinian leader of the radical group Hamas. Members of Hamas have been involved in many terrorist attacks against Israel.

In December 2002, a series of battles between Palestinians and Israeli soldiers left almost 60 people dead. Some were innocent children. One eight-year-old boy died when Israeli soldiers clashed with Palestinians who were throwing stones at them. A girl, age nine, died when she was hit by a bullet while standing outside her home.

Israelis were not only being attacked inside their country but in other areas as well. In November, at an Israeli-owned hotel in Mombasa, Kenya, a terrorist attack killed three Jewish vacationers and eleven Kenyans. Also, an Israeli plane carrying tourists from the Mombasa airport was attacked by missiles and barely escaped being hit. Afterward, the terrorist group Al Qaeda claimed that it had engineered the attacks. This is the same Islamic group that crashed planes into the World Trade Center in New York City and the Pentagon on September 11, 2001.

Sharon has a reputation for being tough with Arab radicals. Many Israelis believe that this is the only way to deal with the Palestinians. As one Israeli political expert put it: Sharon "appears to be the steady hand at the wheel, which is probably why most Israelis also prefer him." The cost has been enormous, however. The Israeli economy has been suffering. Many tourists have stayed away because of the violence. In addition, Israel has suffered from a worldwide recession that has affected high-tech industries and other businesses. Unemployment rose to more than 10 percent in 2002, which is high for Israel. As one expert said, "It's by far the worst recession that Israel has ever had."

The economy is not the major issue for most Israelis, though. As one Israeli pollster explained: "It's like the sixth most-important issue. The first five are security and defense." When Sharon was first elected in 2001, he promised the Israeli people peace and economic security. Yet the cycle of violence between Israel and the Palestinians has only worsened. More than 700 Israelis and more than 2,000 Palestinians died during a 24-month period from 2001 to 2003. Sharon blamed the Palestinian Authority led by Arafat. He has called it "a murderous regime [that] must be removed and replaced with one of peace." Arafat, on the other hand, has accused Sharon of doing everything in his power to prevent the formation of a Palestinian state.

During the year or more leading up to Sharon's re-election, the violence grew especially bloody. On October 17, 2001, Rehavam Zeevi, former Israeli tourism minister, was assassinated in Jerusalem. Zeevi, 75 years old, was a friend of Sharon's. He was shot by Palestinian gunmen at a hotel after eating breakfast. Sharon immediately called a meeting of his cabinet to discuss the situation. Sharon demanded that Arafat turn over the men responsible for the killing, but he refused. A radical Palestinian group said it had carried out the assassination; Arafat had nothing to do with it. It was an act of revenge, the group said, to pay back the Israelis for killing one of its leaders several months earlier.

Sharon, however, had no intention of backing down. "Everything has changed," he said. "The situation is different today, and it will not be like it was yesterday." Israeli tanks began to enter Palestinian towns along the West Bank, hunting for Palestinian terrorists. Battles broke out with the

Palestinians. In response to increased Israeli military activity, Palestinian terrorist attacks continued. In November 2001, two riflemen entered the town of Afula, in northern Israel. They killed two Israelis and wounded many others before being shot to death by the Afula police. Other Palestinian attacks occurred at an Israeli settlement in Gaza, where a woman was killed and a two-year-old infant was wounded. In Tel Aviv, a suicide bomber blew himself up on a bus, killing three passengers.

Late on the evening of December 1, 2001, two suicide bombers sent by Hamas walked into a large shopping center in Jerusalem. Suddenly, there were violent explosions as they blew themselves up. Ten Israeli teenagers were killed and more than 180 people were wounded. The scene was filled with bloodshed and destruction. Less than 12 hours later, another Palestinian suicide bomber took his own life and the lives of 15 other people on a bus in the Israeli city of Haifa.

The Israeli Defense Forces (IDF) struck back rapidly. One of its targets was the airport at Palestinian Authority head-quarters in Gaza City. Jets destroyed the aircraft that Arafat used to fly from town to town in the Palestinian territories. The runways were destroyed so the airport could not be used again. Israeli jets also struck Palestinian towns in the West Bank, where terrorists were thought to be hiding. The IDF hit Arafat's headquarters in the town of Ramallah on the West Bank. Many buildings were destroyed, and Arafat was forced to take refuge in a nearby bomb shelter. Arafat said he feared for his life, but Sharon had no intention of killing him. The prime minister realized that Arafat's death would turn him into a martyr, inflaming the Palestinians further and increasing the violence.

By the middle of December 2001, Israeli leaders announced that they no longer would be able to deal with Arafat. They called him "irrelevant as far as Israel is concerned." Indeed, Arafat seemed to have little or no control over radical groups

In response to Palestinian attacks against Israeli citizens, the Israeli Defense Force has responded with military action. Here, an Israeli tank enters Palestinian territory after the assassination of Israeli tourism minister Rehavam Zeevi in October 2001.

like Hamas, which were continuing to attack Israeli cities. Ten passengers on a bus were killed when Hamas agents set off bombs underneath it and then shot the Israelis as they came out. Some observers, though, believed that Arafat was either engineering the violence or allowing it to happen. This was his way of showing Sharon that he would not back down.

As Arafat put it: "We will remain on the front line until Judgment Day, generation after generation, struggle after struggle. . . . We shall continue our struggle until the flag of Palestine is unfurled over Jerusalem." Palestinians believe that Jerusalem should be the capital of their state. Sharon and other Israelis, however, regard Jerusalem as the capital of Israel.

In February 2002, Sharon traveled to Washington to meet with President George W. Bush. At a news conference, Sharon restated his belief that the Palestinians were entitled to their own state, at least some day. The state would include some parts of the West Bank and Gaza Strip. But Jerusalem would remain in the hands of Israel, which would also control Palestine's foreign affairs and patrol the new nation's borders. Sharon also made it clear that he would not negotiate with Arafat unless the Palestinian violence stopped.

This position was unacceptable to the Palestinians, but Arafat could do little. He remained a prisoner in his bomb shelter in Ramallah. Although Arafat called for an end to the suicide bombings, they continued. In January 2002, Wafa Idris became the first young woman to become a suicide bomber. The 28-year-old woman killed herself and an elderly man and wounded two other Israelis. Many Palestinians hailed her as a martyr and a heroine.

In March, a far more deadly explosion occurred at a hotel in the Israeli city of Netanya. During Passover, an important festival in the Jewish religion, a member of Hamas sneaked into the hotel. Abdel-Basset Odeh, age 23, entered a dining room where Israelis were sitting and set off a bomb. He killed himself and 29 other people; 140 people were injured. Sharon reacted quickly, launching Operation Defense Shield. The IDF tightened the siege of Ramallah, and Arafat was not permitted to leave his headquarters. Israeli soldiers also searched for suspected terrorists. Similar searches were conducted in other West Bank communities, including Nablus, Jenin, and Bethlehem.

In Bethlehem, Palestinian soldiers took refuge inside the Church of the Nativity in April 2002. This was the traditional site that commemorates the birth of Jesus Christ. "We won't surrender, even if all of us are killed," one Palestinian gunman said. The IDF eventually allowed them to leave in May. In the meantime, the IDF clamped curfews on the West Bank towns. People could not go out and get medical help for the wounded or buy food for themselves.

Israeli aggression was met by more violence from the Palestinians. An 18-year-old woman detonated a bomb attached to her at an Israeli supermarket, taking the lives of two other people and wounding 30 shoppers.

Meanwhile, the IDF carried out an attack on the West Bank settlement of Jenin. From this settlement, Hamas had launched more than 25 suicide bombings against Israel. A pitched battle broke out between Israelis and Palestinians on the streets of Jenin. Fighting continued from house to house as Israeli soldiers tried to close in on Palestinian soldiers and terrorists. One man they killed was Mahmoud Tawalbe. He had directed a number of terrorist assaults on Israeli citizens. During the fighting, innocent civilians were also killed. To drive out the Palestinians, the Israelis attacked with helicopters, knocking out enemy positions on the roofs of buildings in Jenin. The IDF also brought in large bulldozers and knocked down buildings in which the Palestinians were hiding.

After the 12-day battle for Jenin ended with an IDF victory, there were reports that Israelis had massacred innocent Palestinians. Later investigations showed that no massacre had occurred. Still, more than 50 Palestinians had been killed, and almost as many were missing. Much of the Palestinian settlement in Jenin was destroyed. During the battle in Jenin, another fierce fight was occurring in Nablus, where 78 people were killed.

In the spring of 2002, the violence continued. In April, a 20-year-old woman named Andaleeb Taqatqa was videotaped explaining why she was a member of the al-Aksa Martyrs Brigade. This is a radical group of suicide bombers with close ties to Arafat. After the videotape was made, she blew herself up at a market in Jerusalem, taking the lives of six people.

Meanwhile, the administration of U.S. President George W. Bush was trying to persuade Israel and the Palestinians to begin peace talks. Sharon finally agreed to allow Arafat to leave his headquarters in Ramallah. Then the prime minister traveled to Washington in May to meet with President Bush. While he was there, however, another massive suicide bombing occurred at a pool hall in Jerusalem. Sixteen people were killed, and many others were wounded. Sharon cut short his meetings in Washington to return to Israel. He described himself as feeling "rage" over the bombing and said, "Israel will react strongly." He added: "Those who fund terrorism are guilty. Those who launch terrorism are guilty—guilty. To anyone who tries to blackmail Israel into making concessions, either big or small through the weapon of terror and fear or tries to blackmail the state of Israel, sowing fear, I say today, Israel will not surrender to blackmail. Israel will not surrender to blackmail."

In June, the IDF struck again at Arafat's headquarters in Ramallah. Many of the remaining buildings were destroyed. The Israeli government was reportedly convinced that Arafat was responsible for the suicide attacks in Israel. The government also accused him of failing to round up those responsible for directing the bombings. Sharon made it clear on more than one occasion that he would like to see Arafat forced out of office or killed. But he assured President Bush that Israel would not harm Arafat. Sharon also feared that pushing Arafat into exile might allow him to gather support from influential people in other parts of the Arab world. In a show of strength, Sharon kept invading Arafat's headquarters. This was Sharon's way of showing the Palestinians how powerless Arafat was, so they might eventually replace him with another leader.

The Israeli government also began to build a fence to separate Israel from some of the West Bank settlements. The fence was largely made out of electrified wire. Video cameras were installed to provide continuous pictures of the area along the fence. With this kind of protection, Israelis hoped to prevent most of the suicide bombers from coming into Israel. A similar fence built along the border between Gaza and Israel, according to the Israeli security agency, has prevented any suicide bombers from attacking from this area.

At the same time, the IDF closed off the main roads on the West Bank. This was to prevent Palestinian gunmen from advancing into Israel or against Israeli settlements on the West Bank. The IDF also occupied northern Gaza. Palestinians who worked in Israel were prevented from returning to their jobs. As a result, about 75 percent of the Palestinian population was out of work in the areas of Gaza occupied by the Israelis.

In July, an Israeli plane bombed an apartment building where the Hamas leader Salah Shehada was thought to be living. Shehada was killed, along with nine innocent children. Another 145 people were wounded. Sharon called Shehada's death "one of our greatest successes." Israel entered a new election season in the fall of 2002 that would lead to Sharon's re-election as prime minister. The suicide attacks had not ended. Nor had Israeli retaliation against Palestinian radicals been reduced. Indeed, the cycle of violence seemed to be growing worse.

Even so, Prime Minister Sharon showed no indication of changing his policies. In fact, his approach to the Palestinian situation remained much the same as it had been for decades. From his earliest days as a military leader, to his years as a politician and finally as prime minister, Sharon has regarded the Palestinians as the enemy. As he once put it, his aim "was to create in the Arabs a psychology of defeat, to beat them every time and to beat them so decisively that they would develop the conviction that they would never win. . . . Only after they've been battered will we be able to conduct talks and reach a peace agreement."

Creating the State of Israel

F or centuries, Israel has been a beacon drawing Jews homeward. The kingdom of Israel was founded on the shores of the Mediterranean Sea around 1000 B.C. by King David. He ruled Israel from his magnificent capital in Jerusalem. David was succeeded by his son Solomon, who strengthened the kingdom and enlarged its territories. After Solomon's death, however, the kingdom broke apart. Israel was conquered again and again by its more powerful neighbors. Eventually, the Romans took control of Jerusalem around 63 B.C. They renamed the area Palestine. When the Jews revolted against Roman authority during the second century A.D., they were expelled from Palestine and scattered throughout the Middle East and Europe. They began their *diaspora,* or dispersion.

In Europe, Jews were regularly persecuted by Christians, who blamed the Jews for the crucifixion and death of Jesus Christ. Some

The city of Jerusalem is considered holy by both Jews and Muslims, which is one reason for the violent struggle for control of the area. The Temple of the Mount and the Dome of the Rock, seen here, are two major Muslim holy sites located in Jerusalem.

Jews escaped and returned to Palestine. By this time, the territory was controlled by Muslims, who were followers of the Prophet Muhammad. The Muslims had occupied Palestine during the seventh century and continued to rule it for more than 1,200 years.

During the nineteenth century, persecutions of the Jews increased. In Russia, for example, mobs attacked Jewish homes and businesses. They were encouraged to make these violent attacks, called pogroms, by the Russian government.

Some Jews escaped the pogroms and traveled to Israel. Meanwhile, a few Jewish leaders in Europe began calling for a homeland for the Jews. This movement, known as Zionism, was led by Theodor Herzl, a Hungarian Jew. Herzl believed that Jews would only be safe from persecution if they had a Jewish state to protect them. As the Zionist movement gathered strength, more and more Jews immigrated to Palestine. By 1914, 85,000 Jews and more than 600,000 Arabs were living there. Palestine was ruled by the Ottoman Empire, from its capital in Constantinople.

During World War I (1914–1918), the Ottoman Empire was defeated by the British and French. After the war, Britain took control of Palestine. Jewish settlers continued to stream into Palestine, establishing farms and businesses. Among the settlers were Samuil and Dvora Scheinerman. Samuil was an ardent Zionist who had attended agricultural college at the University of Tiflis in Russia. Dvora was a medical student. In 1922, the Scheinermans left Russia and traveled to Palestine to avoid persecution.

They settled on land north of Tel Aviv near the Plain of Sharon. The farmland was part of a *moshav* in the settlement of Kfar Malal. In a moshav, each farmer owned property individually, but all the farmers were expected to work together and agree on which crops the entire community should grow. Samuil Scheinerman did not fit into this cooperative effort. Most of the farmers wanted to grow oranges and lemons. Scheinerman, however, insisted on growing avocados and mangoes. When others protested, he went ahead and did what he wanted. Scheinerman also fenced his land to keep it separate from the rest of the moshav, and stood guard over it. As a result, he alienated many of the other farmers.

The Scheinermans had two children. One was a daughter, Dita. Then, in 1928, a son whom they named Ariel was born. (Years later, Ariel would change his name from Scheinerman to Sharon.)

As a child, Ariel recalled, his parents had to struggle to make a living. "At first my parents lived in one room," he wrote,

> a mule and a cow in the other. Inside, the walls were plastered with a mixture of mud, dried manure, and straw. I remember as a child staring at the wall next to my bed, watching the gaps between the studs and the adjoining mud grow wider as time passed. I remember, too, the ceiling rafters that divided the living space from the attic. Big rats made their homes up there, staring down and waiting to jump on any food that my mother might happen to leave in the kitchen.

Growing up, Ariel had a sense of isolation from other children. This feeling was created because his parents and the other children's parents often seemed to disagree. Ariel's mother missed her home in Russia and believed that Russian traditions were superior to anything she had found in Palestine. She sometimes spent an entire day alone in her room, writing to friends back home. Once, when he was five years old, Ariel was thrown off his donkey and cut his chin. Instead of taking him to the local doctor, his mother carried Ariel several miles to a Russian doctor in another village.

As the number of Jewish settlers increased, resentment grew among the Arabs. They regarded Palestine as their territory, not as a homeland for persecuted Jews. Ariel's father carried a pistol. He was forced to use it to protect himself when the Arabs tried to ambush him. During the 1930s, more than 100,000 Jews left Europe for Palestine. They were escaping the rise of the Nazis, who violently persecuted the Jews. Fear mounted among the Arabs that their lands were being taken over by Jews. In 1936, the Arabs began a revolt that included the murder of Jewish farmers.

During the rising tensions of the 1930s, Ariel attended elementary school at Kfar Malal. One fellow student recalled: "I don't remember him ever lying. Sometimes people didn't like what he said, but he always said what he really thought.

In the years that followed World War II, many Jews who had once lived in Europe fled to the land that is now Israel, hoping to create a Jewish homeland in their traditional holy territory. Although many of the migrating Jews, like these, held great hope for the future, they often met with violence upon reaching the Holy Land.

Arik always knew where he was headed. His mother always told him that it was important to be educated and to have a goal. He never sat quietly. Very ambitious."

By 1939, the conflict had grown so intense that the British took decisive action. They substantially reduced the number of Jews permitted to enter Palestine and buy land. That same year, World War II began. Nazi persecutions of the Jews increased, as German soldiers overran most of Europe. The British turned away escaping Jews trying to find refuge in Palestine.

As a result, Jewish people's anger at the British government increased. Jews had formed a volunteer army, called the Haganah, to protect their lands from the Arabs. Some members of the Haganah believed that it should support the British, who were fighting the Nazis during the war. More radical members believed that Jews should oppose the British because they were preventing European refugees from entering Palestine.

At the age of 14, Ariel became a member of the Haganah. Although he believed that the British should be supported in the war against the Nazis, he also admired the Haganah's more radical members who opposed British rule. Some of these radicals were members of the Irgun, led by Menachem Begin, who would later become prime minister of Israel. The Irgun was a militant underground organization that vowed to use any means to end British control of Israel. By the end of the war, the Haganah and the Irgun were working together against the British. In 1946, the Irgun bombed the headquarters of the British administrators of the region at the King David Hotel in Jerusalem, killing more than 90 people.

By this time, the British realized that they could not restore peace in Palestine. They announced plans to withdraw from the area and turned the issue over to the United Nations (UN). The UN had been established at the end of World War II as a peace-keeping body that included many of the world's nations. In 1947, a report from the UN Special Committee on Palestine urged that the area be split between an Arab state and a Jewish state. That same year, the UN voted to approve the formation of a state of Israel.

Although Sharon and other Jews were delighted with this decision, the Arabs were completely opposed to it. Guerrilla warfare increased. As a member of the Haganah, Sharon proved to be a talented guerrilla fighter. He knew the territory around Kfar Malal. He could lead his men across the roads and trails at night, strike an Arab position, and return home before dawn. Arabs and Jews found themselves in a bloody struggle that was called the "Battle of the Roads." The Arabs were trying to cut communications between Jewish settlements by controlling the roads that connected them.

One Arab base near Kfar Malal and other Jewish settlements was Bir Addas. It was a strongly defended position. Early in 1948, Jewish soldiers planned a campaign to capture it. As Sharon recalled, they approached the town on a stormy night with bolts of lightning streaking across the sky. He was expected to lead his battalion—about 40 men—through the darkness so it would be in a position to attack in the morning. Along the way, some of his men became lost, and he had to go back and find them. When the attack finally began, the Arabs were strong enough to beat it back. Eventually, the Jews were forced to retreat without taking their objective. However, the Arabs later decided to abandon their position.

On May 14, 1948, Prime Minister David Ben-Gurion announced that the new state of Israel would be launched at midnight. At the same time, the Arab states in the area intended to invade Israel and try to destroy it. Arab armies from Egypt in the south, Jordan and Iraq in the east, as well as Syria and Lebanon in the north struck the new nation of Israel. The two major Israeli cities of Tel Aviv and Jerusalem were cut off from each other by Arab armies. Ben-Gurion and his advisors decided to attack the city of Latrun—held by Arab soldiers—to reopen the road connecting Jerusalem and Tel Aviv.

Latrun was held by the Jordanians. The Israeli Defense Forces (IDF), which had been created from the old Haganah, planned to march through the night and strike Latrun from several directions. Sharon was expected to lead his platoon and strike the center of the Jordanian force based in an old monastery on a hill. In the early morning hours, the platoon reached a wheat field below the Jordanian position. The field was covered in fog as Sharon and his men moved forward. As morning broke, the fog lifted and suddenly Sharon found himself in the glaring sunlight. His position was heavily attacked by Jordanian machine guns and artillery. His men took cover in a gully, but many were wounded. Sharon himself

Israeli Prime Minister David Ben-Gurion (left) signed the document proclaiming the nation of Israel on May 14, 1948. Many of the surrounding Arab nations immediately set out to destroy the new Jewish state.

took a bullet in the stomach. Eventually, the Israelis were forced to retreat, leaving the Jordanians in control of Latrun.

While Sharon was recuperating in the hospital, the United Nations called a truce in the Palestinian war. During the cease-fire, the IDF strengthened itself with more recruits and arms. Soon the fighting continued, but this time the IDF was successful in pushing back the Arab invaders. When the war finally ended early in 1949, Israel's borders were secure.

After the war, Sharon decided to remain in the army. In

1950, he was appointed an intelligence officer with the branch of the IDF that guarded central Israel. Unfortunately, he had contracted malaria, a disease carried by mosquitoes that causes fevers and chills. The attacks continue unless the malaria is properly treated. Sharon took a leave of absence from the army in 1951. He returned the following year when he was handed an assignment by General Moshe Dayan, one of the leaders of the IDF.

Dayan told him that two Israeli soldiers had been captured by the Jordanians. The general wanted to know if the Israelis could carry out a mission to capture several Jordanian soldiers, who might then be exchanged for the Israeli captives. Sharon thought he could come up with a successful plan. A short time later, Sharon and one of his men approached a Jordanian police station on the banks of a river. They pretended to be Arabic farmers who had lost their cow. When several Jordanian police officers came across the river to help, Sharon and his comrade drew their guns and captured them. The officers could now be exchanged for the Israeli soldiers. "When he found out what had happened," Sharon wrote, "Dayan made no attempt to hide his pleasure. He positively relished the idea that someone would do this kind of thing."

Although he had achieved success in the army, Sharon was not sure it was the career he wanted. Instead, he was considering a different kind of life. Several years earlier, he had met a young woman named Margalit Zimmerman. Nicknamed Gali, she was working as a psychiatric nurse in a Jerusalem hospital. In 1953, Gali and Sharon were married. Meanwhile, he had decided to enroll at Hebrew University and major in Middle Eastern history.

While in college, Sharon remained a member of the army reserves. In the summer of 1953, he received a request to lead a guerrilla expedition against a Jordanian terrorist. He agreed, gathering together a small group of men who had fought with him in the past. In the dark, they slipped into the village where the terrorist lived and put a charge of explosives against the door of his house. The explosives failed to go off, though, and it turned out that the terrorist was not even in the house. Sharon and his men were fortunate to escape without being discovered by Jordanian soldiers.

Sharon was upset that the mission had not been more successful. In his report, he said that Israeli guerrillas had to be much better trained to accomplish such a raid. Unknown to Sharon, his report was sent up the IDF chain of command. A few weeks later, he was asked to form a commando unit to carry out hit-and-run attacks against the Arabs. During the early 1950s, Arab terrorist activities against Israel had increased. In 1951, almost 140 Israeli settlers were killed in attacks from Egypt and Jordan. This number had grown to more than 160 by 1953. So far, the IDF had not trained commandos who could retaliate successfully.

Sharon recruited a small group of volunteers for the new group, which he called Commando Unit 101. The training was rigorous. As one historian wrote:

> Each soldier had to be in perfect physical condition to be able to walk thirty miles in one night, loaded down with equipment; to throw grenades accurately from various distances in a variety of situations; to operate in the dark as easily as in daylight; to slip soundlessly by enemy guards; to freeze under fire and to hold his fire. Each had to know how to handle a knife and to kill with it, to fight hand to hand, to learn the topographical details of every terrain, to be aware of his surroundings at all times so that he would not stray or lose his way. . . .

Sharon led his men into Arab territory. He ordered them to observe the enemy but do nothing, then leave quietly without being detected. This would train them to operate effectively. Finally, his group of 45 men appeared ready for an actual mission. The first target was a Palestinian refugee camp located

To protect themselves in the ongoing struggle against neighboring Arab countries, Israelis formed military groups, such as Haganah, some of whose recruits are seen here. By training young men to fight, Israel hoped to maintain the independence and security of the new nation.

in the Gaza Strip, between Egypt and Israel along the Mediterranean Sea. Many Palestinians had fled there during the 1948 war. From the refugee camps, Arab *fedayeen,* or militants, were trained to infiltrate Israel and carry out raids. Sharon's first mission was not entirely successful. His men attacked the refugee camp at night and found themselves in a pitched battle with the fedayeen. They were fortunate to escape with only light casualties.

In the fall of 1953, Sharon launched another commando raid, as a reprisal for an Arab attack on the home of a Jewish woman and her children. The Arabs had thrown a grenade through a window, killing all of them. The attack had been launched from the Palestinian village of Kibbiya in Jordan, near the Israeli border. Sharon's men assaulted the village, killing the Arab guards. Then the Israeli commandos called the residents out of their homes and began to blow up the buildings. It was a successful raid. Later, however, Sharon learned that more than 60 civilians had remained inside their homes and been killed. Although he was saddened by the deaths, Sharon also believed that the attack had achieved its purpose. As he wrote: "While the civilian deaths were a tragedy, the Kibbiya raid was also a turning point. After . . . many defeats . . . it was now clear that Israeli forces were capable of finding and hitting targets far behind enemy lines. What this meant to army morale can hardly be exaggerated."

As a result of Sharon's success, General Dayan asked him to train more commandos. Dayan ordered the Israeli paratroopers and Unit 101 to work together under Sharon's command. Sharon's training efforts increased. At first, the paratroopers were physically unable to match the commandos. Gradually, they increased their ability to march long distances and carry heavy equipment. Each time they were sent out on patrol, they would file "post-action reports." These would be carefully analyzed by Sharon and his officers to find out where improvements could be made so raids could become more effective.

Meanwhile, the IDF ordered the commandos to switch from civilian to enemy military targets. Some of the commandos had been upset about having to kill civilians. As one historian wrote: "As a result of this tactical change, even . . . Arab commentators acknowledged that villages were no longer being targeted. The commandos developed a new sense of pride: They could display captured weapons to international visitors and bask in the praise their accomplishments generated."

In February 1955, the commandos struck a heavily defended position in the Gaza Strip, which was controlled by Egypt. The position was occupied by Egyptian soldiers who had fortified two military camps. The Israelis attacked in the darkness, killing many enemy soldiers who were caught by surprise, and blowing up military buildings. Then they retreated.

The attack against the Egyptian position helped convince President Gamal Abdel Nasser of Egypt that he needed more powerful weapons to do battle with the Israelis. In 1955, Nasser made a deal with the Soviet Union to sell the Soviets cotton and rice in return for fighter planes, tanks, and other arms. Meanwhile, Sharon's raids against the Egyptians continued. Late in 1955, his men struck the Egyptian fortress of Kuntilla under cover of darkness. They captured almost 30 prisoners, then retreated. Between 1954 and 1956, according to Sharon, his unit conducted 70 raids against the Arab states.

In 1956, President Nasser decided to take control of the Suez Canal. This waterway, located in northern Egypt, connected the Mediterranean and the Red seas. The canal was owned by France and Great Britain and used as a primary route for shipping oil from the Middle East to Europe. The British and the French decided to retake the canal with the help of Israel. Plans called for the IDF to take a position at the Mitla Pass in the Sinai Desert near the entrance to the Suez Canal. Then France and Britain would land paratroopers in the area and recapture the canal from the Egyptians.

The Israeli invasion began at the end of October. IDF paratroopers were airlifted to the Mitla Pass, 120 miles behind the Egyptian lines. Meanwhile, Sharon was ordered to lead his men across the Sinai Desert from Israel to link up with the paratroopers. By October 31, Sharon had reached the Mitla Pass. He decided to march into the pass, not realizing that the Egyptians had taken up positions in the cliffs there. General Dayan gave him permission to place a small contingent of soldiers there. But Sharon disobeyed orders and marched in with a much larger force. Since he had not scouted the pass, he was surprised by the Egyptians.

Sharon's men found themselves under fire. Although Sharon eventually won the battle, his casualties were very heavy. In the meantime, other Israeli forces had driven the Egyptian army out of the Sinai and taken control of the area as well as the Gaza Strip. Nevertheless, worldwide opinion was opposed to the war. The United States pressured Britain and France to leave the canal after their invasion. The Israelis were also forced to pull back from their positions in Gaza and the Sinai.

Sharon was unhappy about the Israeli withdrawal. He believed that the IDF victories had eliminated a serious terrorist threat. Now the Israelis might be forced to deal with that threat again. A UN peacekeeping force took over patrols along the Sinai and the Gaza Strip. War had ended for Sharon. For the next ten years, he would find himself playing a different role in the Israeli army.

3

War
After War

riel Sharon was severely criticized by General Dayan for disobeying orders at the Mitla Pass. Still, he continued to command his parachute brigade. In 1957, Sharon was sent to England for additional training. When he returned, he was appointed head of an infantry training school. This was a demotion, and Sharon felt that he had been removed from the IDF leadership. He remained in this position for the next four years. Sharon also returned to school part-time and eventually received a law degree.

In 1962, tragedy unexpectedly struck the Sharon family. Gali was driving a small sports car on her way to work at the Ministry of Health in Jerusalem when she was killed in an automobile accident. Sharon was suddenly a single parent with a five-year-old boy, Gur. He received help raising Gur from Gali's sister, Lily. Gradually, a close

Ariel Sharon is seen here with his wife, Lily, whom he married in 1963. Lily was a major source of support in her husband's political career.

relationship developed between Sharon and Lily, leading to their marriage in 1963.

As Sharon's personal life became happier, promotions also came his way. In 1963, he was appointed chief of staff of the army defending the northern sector of Israel—called the

Northern Command. Sharon served under General Yitzhak Rabin, the commander-in-chief. Two years later, Rabin appointed him a major general.

While Sharon's career was improving, though, relations between Israel and the Arab states were growing steadily worse. Syria had decided to begin a new project that would prevent vital water supplies in the Jordan River from reaching Israel. The IDF attacked it, leading to a series of skirmishes along the Syrian border. Syria bombarded Jewish farms, and the Israeli government retaliated by sending planes against the Syrian gun positions. The Syrians called on President Nasser of Egypt for help.

Along Israel's southern border, war was drawing closer with the Egyptians. In May 1967, Nasser ordered the United Nations soldiers patrolling the Gaza Strip and Sinai Desert to leave. He also closed the Straits of Tiran, the entrance to the Red Sea from the Gulf of Aqaba. Israeli ships had to sail from the gulf through the Straits of Tiran to reach the Red Sea. The route was the only way they could reach ports on the east coast of Africa, India, and southern Asia.

The Israeli government regarded Nasser's actions as the first step in starting a war. The Egyptians were supported by other Arab states, including Jordan, Syria, and Iraq. Israeli Prime Minister Levi Eshkol feared that the IDF might be overwhelmed by the combined Arab armies. He believed that the army should take only limited action. He urged the military commanders to take control of Gaza, then trade it to Egypt for the reopening of the Straits of Tiran. Sharon, however, said this response was far too mild. Along with other military leaders, he urged the prime minister to launch a massive strike against Egypt before it could begin a war. Sharon was convinced that the IDF was more than a match for the Arab armies and could defeat them on the battlefield.

On June 3, 1967, Eshkol and the military commanders finally agreed on a so-called preemptive strike. On the morning of June 5, Israeli planes took off and headed for Egypt. They flew low to avoid detection by Egyptian radar. A few hours later, they reached Egyptian airfields and began to destroy almost 300 enemy planes that sat on the runways waiting to take off. It was a bold, decisive strike that knocked the Egyptian air force out of the war before it could attack Israel.

Meanwhile, Sharon and other IDF commanders were planning to lead their tank divisions southward through the Sinai. The night before the attack began, Sharon wrote a letter to his wife, Lily, who was worried about his safety. "You have to understand," he told her, "the most important thing is that the battle will be in the hands of the most experienced commanders, and that's why it's important that I be here. . . . I will take care of myself because I know about the wonderful things that await me at home."

The next day, one Israeli force struck along the coast, capturing the key Egyptian positions at Rafah and El Arish in the Sinai. In the center of the Sinai, Sharon led his division against the key Egyptian stronghold at Abu Agheila. The assault began under the cover of darkness. Some of Sharon's men attacked the entrenched enemy from the front, while other Israeli soldiers struck from the rear. By the following morning, they had overrun the Egyptian positions and taken control of Abu Agheila. The Egyptians also began to evacuate other strongholds in the desert, including Keussaima and Nakhel. The Egyptian army was retreating rapidly through the Mitla Pass and back to the Suez Canal.

At the pass, however, the Egyptians were caught by rapidly advancing Israeli army units. After Sharon finally arrived, he recalled: "The scene now was indescribable. The entire pass was choked with the wreckage of the Egyptian army. Tanks, artillery . . . countless hundreds of vehicles smoldered and burned, sending up a black haze that hung like dirty gauze in the clear desert sky." The IDF did not stop, however. Israeli units raced on until they reached the Suez Canal. In the meantime, Israel

Sharon gained valuable military experience fighting in the Six-Day War in 1967. He is seen here at center as an Israeli army general.

had achieved the same success on other fronts. Israeli planes had knocked out the Jordanian air force at the beginning of the war. This enabled the IDF to march eastward and take control of all of Jerusalem (half of it had been part of Jordan) as well as the West Bank of the Jordan River. In the north, IDF troops pushed back the Syrians and captured the Golan Heights.

In six days, the war was over—hence, its name became the "Six-Day War." Israel had tripled its size, and the Arab armies had been decisively defeated. The Israeli government had to decide how to defend the captured territory. Israeli leaders believed that this land was essential for the nation's defense. By occupying the Golan Heights and the West Bank, the Israelis could prevent Arab artillery from firing into the central areas of Israel. In addition, most Israelis regarded Jerusalem and the territory on the West Bank as part of the ancient Jewish homelands.

After the war, Sharon was asked to take charge of all

military training for the IDF. To secure the territory on the West Bank, Sharon moved the Israeli training schools there, establishing them in former Jordanian strongholds. As a result, IDF troops now patrolled the areas from which Jordanian soldiers had once threatened Israel. Although Sharon was involved with his military duties, he still had time to spend with his family. He now had three children—Gur, from his marriage to Gali, and Omri and Gilad, from his marriage to Lily.

One afternoon in the fall of 1967, while Sharon was at home, Gur was playing outside. Suddenly, Sharon heard a shot. He ran out of the house and saw ten-year-old Gur lying on the ground with blood pouring from his head. Gur and another boy had been playing with an old rifle, without realizing it was loaded. Sharon rushed his son to the hospital, but the wound was far too serious and Gur died. Sharon and his wife were heartbroken.

Later, Sharon wrote that while he stood at his son's grave, "I remembered five and a half years ago when we had buried Gali. I had given a brief talk then, and it came back to me that I had said, 'The only thing I can promise you is that I will take care of Gur.' Now I could not shake the thought that I had not kept my promise."

While Sharon was dealing with this personal tragedy, top Israeli military officials were debating the most effective ways to defend the Sinai region along the Suez Canal. Here, a War of Attrition had begun. President Nasser announced: "We shall weaken Israel and damage its ability to withstand our push to regain our captured territory. We will kill soldiers and civilians alike. . . ." Already the killing had begun, with Egyptian and Israeli soldiers firing at each other in the Suez area.

IDF Chief of Staff General Chaim Bar-Lev believed that the best way to defend the Israeli position was to build a line of fortified posts along the canal. Other generals supported him. Sharon, however, believed that the so-called Bar-Lev line was an enormous mistake. He was convinced that a static defense line would not make the maximum use of Israel's powerful tank force. Instead, he proposed that the IDF defend the nearby hills and mountains. Then, the tanks could swoop down against any Egyptian advance, no matter where it occurred. Sharon was very outspoken about his position, so much so that he offended many of his colleagues. General Bar-Lev wanted to force Sharon out of the army, but Sharon made it clear that he would not go quietly. He intended to enter politics and join a political party opposed to the Labor Party that ran the Israeli government. Sharon was very popular in Israel because of his success in the Six-Day War. If he joined the opposition, the power of the Labor Party might decline. Therefore, Labor Party leaders convinced Bar-Lev and Sharon to patch up their differences.

In December 1969, Sharon took over the Southern Command. He directed the forces responsible for guarding the Sinai along the border with Egypt, the Negev region along the border with Jordan, as well as the Gaza Strip. The War of Attrition was growing more intense. Israeli planes were raiding positions inside Egypt. The Egyptians were using surface-to-air missiles, which they had received from the Soviets, to shoot down Israeli aircraft.

In the Negev, Israeli settlements were being struck by Arab commandos from Jordan. Many of these commandos belonged to the Palestine Liberation Organization (PLO). The PLO had been established in 1964 and was later recognized by the Arab states as the "sole, legitimate representative of the Palestinian people." The PLO was dedicated to regaining the land occupied by Israel for Palestinian settlers. Led by its chairman, Yasir Arafat, the PLO did not recognize the state of Israel and vowed to destroy it.

Beginning in 1965, the PLO operated from Jordan. One of its bases was the town of Safi across the Jordanian border. In March 1970, Sharon led a raid on Safi, drove out the PLO, and took control of the town. He also increased patrols along the border to seal it against other PLO attacks.

Yasir Arafat, the leader of the Palestinian Liberation Organization, is seen here in a 1967 photograph. Because Palestinians believed the land granted to Israel after World War II was rightly theirs, they refused for many years to recognize the existence of the Jewish state.

To help him, Sharon enlisted Bedouin tribesmen who lived in the Negev. The Bedouins are nomads with herds of camels and sheep who had traveled in the Negev for centuries. Sharon knew that they were expert trackers who could follow the trail of PLO commandos after they had attacked Israeli settlements. The Bedouins generally traveled on their camels. When these proved too slow, Sharon loaded the camels in large open jeeps, which moved the camels more quickly to places where commando tracks had been found by Israeli soldiers. Then the

Bedouins could pick up the trail and follow it to the PLO camps. The Bedouins were very effective in enabling the IDF to cut down on PLO raids in the Negev.

Meanwhile, Sharon also struck at PLO commandos in the Gaza Strip. Here he assigned IDF units to small sections of the Gaza communities. In many cases, PLO commandos were hiding in Arab houses. The IDF went house to house, searching for the guerrillas. Israeli soldiers also carried rope ladders that enabled them to climb up on courtyard walls surrounding Arab houses. They could look over the walls to see if any PLO guerrillas might be holed up inside. Eventually, the guerrillas were forced to give up their hiding places. Some were killed by the IDF in gun battles on the Gaza streets. Other guerrillas tried to conceal themselves in underground bunkers hidden among the Arab orange groves in the Gaza Strip. However, the IDF looked for pipes coming up through the ground that provided air to the hideouts. Then it would launch an attack against the PLO bunkers.

Sharon reported that between July 1971 and February 1972, the IDF killed more than 100 terrorists and arrested more than 700 others. Sharon's methods were not always supported by other top Israeli commanders. They pointed out that Arab bystanders had been hurt while Sharon was attacking the PLO terrorists. In addition, they said Arab civilians had been roughly treated by Sharon as he questioned them to learn the whereabouts of hidden commandos. Nevertheless, according to Sharon, his strategy virtually eliminated the power of the PLO in the Gaza Strip.

In the south, along the Egyptian border, the conflict had also been reduced. A cease-fire had gone into effect in 1970. Shortly afterward, President Nasser died of a heart attack and was replaced by Anwar Sadat. During the cease-fire, however, Sadat began to strengthen his forces along the Suez Canal. The Egyptian army built a large wall and began to mass its forces behind it. Sadat's intention was to drive the Israelis back from the Suez Canal and regain control of the Sinai Desert. To keep the Israelis off balance, the Syrians would strike from the north and push the IDF back from the Golan Heights.

Israeli intelligence was aware of an Egyptian buildup. However, the IDF was confident that it could repeat the victory of 1967 if war should break out. Sadat also tried to confuse the Israelis. He repeatedly put his soldiers on alert, as if a war were about to begin, then put them on standby. After a while, the Israeli high command began to disregard the Egyptian maneuvers.

Sharon was more fearful of an eventual war than many of his colleagues. But in 1973, he had left active duty with the IDF. The army high command wanted its senior officers to retire by the age of 45, to leave openings for younger men in the top positions. With financial help from a friend, Sharon bought a large farm in the Negev. He moved Lily and his children there and became a farmer, just like his father.

Sharon also became interested in politics again. He decided that a coalition of small political parties might successfully challenge the powerful Labor Party and eventually win control of the government. Because of his popularity in Israel, Sharon believed that he might be just the right person to lead such a coalition. The most important politician he had to convince was Menachem Begin, who led the Herut Party. Begin had a long history in Israeli politics. He had participated in the independence movement, which led to the establishment of Israel in 1948. He disagreed with the policies of the Labor Party, though, and had established his own party. Begin lived a very simple life in a small apartment with little furniture. He devoted himself to politics and the policies in which he believed.

In 1973, Begin and Sharon decided to work together to bring the small opposition parties together in a coalition known as Likud. The Likud Party would run candidates for the Israeli Knesset in the election in November. Sharon agreed to work as the campaign manager for Likud and run for a seat in the Knesset.

During the 1973 Yom Kippur War, Sharon held a position of responsibility. Seen here with a bandaged head, he confers with former army chief of staff Haim Bar-Lev about military strategy.

Before the election season was fully under way, however, Egyptian troops attacked across the Suez Canal. President Sadat had decided to launch his assault on October 6, 1973. This was the most solemn holy day in the Jewish religion, Yom Kippur. Sadat reasoned that the Israelis would be completely involved in the religious holiday and could be taken by surprise. The Israeli government, led by Prime Minister Golda Meir, had some advance intelligence warning that the Egyptians might be about to start another war. Meir even considered a preemptive strike, like the one that had been launched in 1967. She believed that Israel's strong ally, the United States, might not support such action, however. Instead, she called up the reserve forces of the IDF and kept them ready in case an Egyptian attack should begin.

Sharon, who was still a member of the reserves, was ordered to report back to the Southern Command. Before Sharon or any of the other IDF troops could reach the Sinai, however, the Egyptians struck. With 100,000 soldiers, they easily overran the Bar-Lev line, which was only lightly defended. Sharon had been right—the fortifications were not enough to stop a massive assault backed up by Egyptian tanks. At the same time, the Syrians struck from the north. They sent 600 tanks against the IDF, which had only 177 tanks, and pushed back the soldiers holding the Golan Heights position.

Sharon rushed to the Sinai, where he found himself serving under a new commanding officer, General Shmuel Gonen. The IDF tried to hold back the Egyptians by sending in the few tanks that were already in the Sinai, but the effort was too little to do any good. The Egyptians were far more powerful and drove them northward. As the IDF tanks retreated, Sharon said he

> stopped some of them to talk to the officers and saw something strange on their faces—not fear but bewilderment. Suddenly something was happening to them that had not happened before. These were soldiers . . . brought up on victories. . . . It was a generation that had never lost. Now they were in a state of shock. How could it be that these Egyptians were crossing the canal right in our faces? How was it that *they* were moving forward and *we* were defeated?

The Israeli high command planned to stop the Egyptian advance by flank attacks. One would come from the north, and the other, led by Sharon, would come from the south. The attack from the north failed, however. Just in time, Sharon's attack was called off, and he retreated to a position along the hills east of the Suez Canal. Some of these hills had been captured by the Egyptians, and Sharon had to fight hard to regain them. From this position, he prepared to hold off a massive Egyptian tank attack. The battle pitted more than 2,000 Egyptian and Israeli tanks against each other. As the Egyptians moved forward, though, they lost the protection of their heavy artillery stationed in the rear. The IDF destroyed about 250 Egyptian tanks, while the Israelis reportedly lost only six tanks.

While the Egyptians were attacking, Sharon had noticed an opening between two of their armies. Once the assault was beaten back, Sharon was given permission to advance through the opening toward the canal. In a lightning advance begun on October 15, his men moved to the Suez Canal and crossed it. The battle against the Egyptian defenders was fierce. "Here and there," Sharon wrote,

> Israeli and Egyptian tanks had destroyed each other at a distance of a few [yards], barrel to barrel. It was as if a hand-to-hand battle of armor had taken place. And inside those tanks and next to them lay their dead crews. Coming close, you could see Egyptian and Jewish dead lying side by side, soldiers who had jumped from their burning tanks and had died together.

Sharon was victorious, and more than 150 Egyptian tanks were destroyed. Sharon's troops were now able to come in behind one of the Egyptian armies and cut it off. However, the IDF command feared that Sharon himself was being surrounded by the Egyptians, and ordered him not to advance any farther. Indeed, his superiors later reprimanded him for advancing too far on the Egyptian side of the canal.

On October 22, the United Nations asked the Arabs and Israelis to begin a cease-fire, which was backed by the United

States and the Soviet Union, the world's two superpowers. The Americans supported Israel, while the Soviets supported Egypt and Syria. Under the terms of a peace agreement, signed early in 1974, the IDF pulled back across the Suez Canal to a position 20 miles (32 kilometers) to the east. The Egyptian army that had been surrounded was permitted to free itself. On the border with Syria, the Israelis had pushed back the Syrian troops across the Golan Heights during the war. As a result of the peace agreement, Israel held on to vital defensive positions on the Syrian border.

Sharon was bitter about the agreement. He also criticized the performance of the IDF high command during the war. In a speech to his troops who had successfully crossed the canal, he said:

> We must remember that our victory in the Yom Kippur War was the greatest of all other victories. . . . despite the blunders and the mistakes, despite the failures and obstructions, despite the loss of control and authority, we nevertheless achieved our victory, we must therefore recognize that this was the greatest victory the IDF has ever known.

The IDF leadership was very angry that Sharon would openly criticize its performance. Even so, the speech was widely publicized in Israel, and he stood by it. Ariel Sharon was never afraid to speak his mind. He did not care if others disagreed with him.

Sharon, the Politician

Ariel Sharon realized that he did not have a bright future in the
army. After criticizing the high command, there was little
chance he would be promoted. Therefore, he left active duty
in the IDF to focus his attention on politics. In the elections held in
December 1973, many Israelis voted against the Labor Party. They
blamed it for mishandling the war. The Likud Party won seats in the
Knesset, although it did not gain a majority. One of the new parlia-
mentary members was Sharon.

Sharon found that the Knesset was quite different from the army.
In parliament, he was supposed to work with other members of the
Likud to create new laws. This involved compromise, which Sharon
found difficult. He grew impatient with the need for meetings and
discussions with other politicians to create legislation. Sharon was far
more interested in action than conversation.

During the years he served as Israeli prime minister, Yitzhak Rabin (right) relied heavily on the advice of Ariel Sharon (left), who was a special consultant on matters of defense.

In 1974, Prime Minister Golda Meir, leader of the Labor Party, resigned. A special commission had severely criticized her leadership during the Yom Kippur War. She was replaced by Yitzhak Rabin, who was an old friend of Sharon's. He invited Sharon to return to active duty in the army and help improve its performance. Sharon accepted and gave up his seat in the Knesset. Soon after his return, Sharon submitted a plan for guarding the new Israeli borders established by the peace agreement after the war. The plan, however, was not accepted by the IDF high command. Sharon was so upset that he openly criticized the decision to other high-ranking officers. "See [their] plan?" he said. "Only an idiot could produce a plan like that!" Other officers were amazed that he would say these things.

Rabin, however, respected Sharon's ability as a military strategist. In 1975, Rabin appointed him as a special advisor on defense matters. Sharon remained in this position for less than a year. He hoped that it would eventually lead to a top leadership role in the IDF. When this did not happen, Sharon resigned.

In 1976, Sharon formed a new political party called *Shlomzion*—Peace for Zion. He hoped to attract other small parties to Shlomzion. In this way, Sharon believed he might form an alternative to Likud and Labor. A major plank of the Shlomzion Party platform was achieving peace with the Palestinians. Sharon believed this would be possible by urging them to return to Jordan. He hoped that the PLO would overthrow the government of King Hussein of Jordan and take control of Jordan as a new Palestinian state. Sharon, though, quickly discovered that the leaders of other small Israeli parties were not interested in joining him. He realized that his best chance to achieve political power was to rejoin Likud.

In 1977, Israel held another general election. This time, Likud defeated the Labor Party, and Menachem Begin became prime minister. He asked Sharon to join his cabinet as minister of agriculture. Begin also put him in charge of new settlements on the West Bank, which Israel had conquered during the 1967 war. Sharon and Begin believed strongly that the West Bank should always remain a part of Israel. Like other Israelis, they called this area Samaria and Judea, the ancient biblical names of these Jewish territories. Sharon was convinced that the territory could only be defended if Jews were encouraged to build settlements there. He was especially interested in locating the settlements in the hills of the West Bank. These hills looked down on the rest of Israel. If they were retaken by Arabs, Sharon feared, Israel might be left wide open to attack.

In addition to the territory on the West Bank, Sharon and Begin were also concerned about the future of Jerusalem. Israel now controlled the entire city. However, many Arabs had migrated there since the Six-Day War. Jerusalem was a thriving city with many job opportunities for the Arabs, whose population there doubled. To retain control of Jerusalem, Sharon suggested that a ring of new Jewish settlements be built around the city. In this way, the Arab immigrants would be cut off from Jordan. This would strengthen the Jewish defense of Jerusalem. The Israeli cabinet accepted Sharon's plan, and new Jewish settlements began to be built.

Meanwhile, an astonishing event occurred that would change the relationship between Israel and Egypt. After negotiations between the two countries, Egyptian President Anwar Sadat came to Israel in November 1977—the first time an Egyptian leader had traveled to the Jewish nation. Sadat came to meet Begin and deliver a speech to the Knesset. In his address, Sadat said: "I come to you today on solid ground to shape a new life and to establish peace. . . . Any life that is lost in war is a human life, be it that of an Arab or an Israeli. . . . Conceive with me a peace agreement . . . that we can herald to a world thirsting for peace." Sadat made it clear that he wanted to end the conflict between Israel and Egypt that had resulted in four wars and thousands of deaths.

Sadat had done what no other Arab leader had dared to do. He had opened the door to peace with Israel. Even so, there was still broad disagreement between the two sides. The Egyptians, for example, wanted to take back control of the Sinai, which had been lost during the 1967 war. The Israelis did not want to allow Egyptian troops back into the Sinai. Nor did they want to tear down the Jewish settlements built there. Sadat also wanted territory set aside to create a state for the Palestinians. The Israeli government opposed such a state.

In Washington, D.C., U.S. President Jimmy Carter committed himself to achieving peace in the Middle East. In the midst of the deadlock between Egypt and Israel, he invited Sadat and Begin to the United States. He proposed to meet with the two men at Camp David, the presidential retreat in Maryland. In September 1978, the leaders of Egypt and Israel along with their advisors arrived at Camp David.

Sadat and Begin met for ten days. President Carter made every effort to bring the two men to an agreement, but they remained far apart. Sadat prepared to leave and return to Egypt. President Carter was very frustrated. He went to Sadat. "I told Sadat," Carter later wrote, "that he had betrayed me, had betrayed our friendship, and had violated the commitment he had made that he would give me every opportunity to resolve any differences that arose. . . . I made my statement as strongly as I could. Sadat was taken aback, then told me that he would stay and give me another chance."

President Carter then went to Begin, who was staying in a different part of Camp David. Carter recalled:

> Begin had asked me to sign some photographs of me, him, and Sadat for his grandchildren. I got the names of his grandchildren and personalized every photograph [with their names]. . . . I handed him the photographs, and, as he looked down, he began calling out the names of his grand-children. His voice trembled, and there were tears running down his cheeks. Then he said, "We can't leave a war for these little children to fight!"

Sadat, Begin, and Carter went back to the bargaining table.

Ariel Sharon was not present at the peace conference. Begin

History was made in the Arab-Israeli conflict when Egyptian President Anwar Sadat (left) and Israeli Prime Minister Menachem Begin (right) signed a peace treaty between their countries after a series of negotiations sponsored by U.S. President Jimmy Carter (center).

stayed in touch with him, however, because he valued Sharon's opinion. Begin told him that Israel must withdraw completely from the Sinai to obtain peace with Egypt. Although Sharon was not in favor of removing the Israeli army or the settlements from the Sinai, he believed that Begin should agree to it if this were the only way to secure peace. Over the next two days, there was a breakthrough. Eventually, the Egyptian and Israeli leaders came to a peace agreement, which was finalized in 1979. Israel agreed to withdraw from the Sinai. In return, Egypt recognized the state of Israel. President Sadat became the first Arab head of state to grant recognition to Israel.

While negotiations continued, Sharon built new settlements on the West Bank. The Egyptian-Israeli agreement had included no specific words about a Palestinian homeland. The Palestinians, meanwhile, raided Israeli settlements from Lebanon, the new home of the PLO headquarters. (The Jordanian army had forced the PLO out of Jordan in 1971 after a Palestinian attempt to assassinate King Hussein.) Early in 1978, Palestinian terrorists killed an American photographer along the coast south of Lebanon. Then they stopped a bus and killed 35 Jews, while wounding 100 others. The IDF retaliated with an invasion of Lebanon. It struck PLO positions and occupied a zone about six miles (ten kilometers) wide inside Lebanon. The zone was designed to keep PLO terrorists from invading northern Israel and killing Jewish settlers.

For centuries, Lebanon had both a large Muslim and Christian population. Christians and Muslims shared power in the government, but there was conflict between these groups. Early in the 1970s, when the PLO left Jordan, it was welcomed into Lebanon by the Muslims but opposed by the Christians. A civil war eventually began between the Christians and the Muslims, who were supported by the PLO. In 1976, Syria invaded Lebanon to end the civil war. The Syrians occupied positions in the eastern part of the country, the Bekaa Valley, as well as in part of Beirut.

The civil war in Lebanon continued. PLO terrorists also traveled across the Israeli border, killing Jewish farmers throughout the late 1970s. While the Israeli government tried to halt the PLO terrorist activities, Sharon and Begin continued to expand Jewish settlements on the West Bank. Both men regarded the Jews who established these settlements as brave pioneers—men and women who were willing to build homes, start businesses, and set up farms on the Israeli frontiers. Besides these settlers, others were moving into the Gaza Strip as well as the Galilee—a sparsely settled area in northern Israel near the Lebanese border.

Sharon believed that all of these people had to be protected — no matter what it took. In 1981, he supported a decision by

Prime Minister Begin to launch an attack on Iraq. The Iraqi government of Saddam Hussein had developed a nuclear reactor that would enable it to develop nuclear weapons. Hussein had made it clear in the past that he thought the state of Israel should be destroyed. Early in June 1981, Begin ordered the Israeli air force to bomb the reactor. As the planes arrived over the reactor, located near Baghdad, the capital of Iraq, they dropped their bombs and quickly destroyed the reactor. None of the planes was hit by Iraqi missiles. The United States and other Western powers criticized the Israelis for the attack. But Begin and Sharon were convinced it was the only way to prevent Saddam Hussein from using nuclear weapons on Israel.

Shortly after the attack on Iraq, Israelis went to the polls for another election. Once again Likud defeated the Labor Party. Begin continued to lead the government, and he asked Sharon to become defense minister. Sharon's primary concern was the situation in Lebanon. According to historian Avi Shlaim, Sharon wanted to remove the PLO from Lebanon. He believed that the best way to do this was with a military alliance between Israel and a powerful Christian leader named Bashir Gemayel. Although the Christians were not united, Gemayel led a strong militia group known as the Phalange. It had been started by his father, Pierre Gemayel. Sharon hoped that with Israel's military backing, Bashir Gemayel might be elected president of Lebanon. Then he would sign a peace treaty with Israel and help the IDF drive out the PLO from Lebanon.

Shlaim believes Sharon realized that the entire Israeli cabinet would not go along with such a plan. The cabinet knew that the United States, Israel's primary ally, was opposed to an Israeli invasion of Lebanon in support of Gemayel. However, Sharon hoped that he could get the cabinet's approval for making small advances into Lebanon. Each advance, he reasoned, would be met by a PLO attack, and the IDF could then retaliate with even stronger force and more advances.

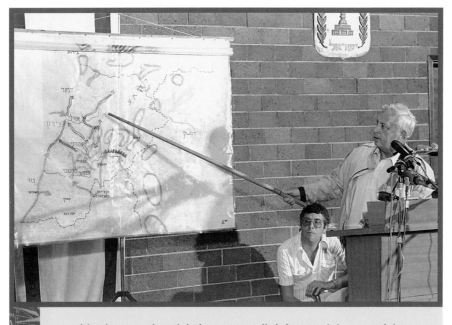

In this photograph, Ariel Sharon, Israeli defense minister, explains his strategy for the 1982 military action against Lebanon, Operation Peace for Galilee.

On June 3, 1982, the Israeli ambassador to England was gravely wounded in an assassination attempt. The assailants were not members of the PLO. They belonged to a more radical Arab group. However, Begin was not concerned about which Palestinian group had committed the attack. He believed the time had come to retaliate against the PLO in Lebanon. On June 5, Israeli planes struck PLO positions in Beirut and in southern Lebanon. In retaliation, the PLO bombarded Israeli settlements in the Galilee. Sharon spoke to the cabinet and urged its members to approve an IDF advance on southern Lebanon and the occupation of a 25-mile-wide (40-kilometer-wide) strip of territory. Sharon also hoped that an IDF invasion would persuade the Syrians to leave the Bekaa Valley. Begin agreed, and the Israeli cabinet supported the new operation, called Operation Peace for Galilee.

IDF forces invaded on June 6. They rapidly swept up the coast, capturing Lebanese towns along the way. Eastward, the IDF and Syrian troops were involved in a fierce battle around the town of Jezzine. The Syrians brought surface-to-air missiles into Lebanon to help beat back the Israeli air force. Sharon obtained the government's approval to strike back. A massive Israeli air strike destroyed the missiles and shot down 23 Syrian jets. The IDF continued to advance northward. At this point, however, the United States stepped in to arrange a cease-fire between Israel and Syria. Nevertheless, the IDF kept advancing, violating the cease-fire, until it surrounded Beirut. Then Sharon unleashed an enormous artillery attack against the PLO positions.

During the summer, the United States continued to put pressure on Begin. Eventually, he agreed to allow U.S. forces to transport the PLO and its leader, Yasir Arafat, out of Lebanon to Tunisia. In August, with Israeli military support, Bashir Gemayel was elected president of Lebanon. But he was assassinated less than a month later, most likely by the Syrians. In response, the IDF expanded its control of Beirut. In addition, it permitted the Phalange militia to enter two Palestinian refugee camps, Sabra and Shatila, located in Beirut.

The mission of the Phalange militia was to remove any PLO soldiers who remained in the camps. What followed, however, was a massacre of innocent men, women, and children. The massacre continued from September 16 to September 19, 1982. As many as 2,000 people may have been killed. Once the massacre became known in Israel, a commission was appointed to investigate. A report from the commission early in 1983 stated that the army had allowed the Phalange to enter the refugee camps and stood by while the militia murdered the Palestinians. The commission held Ariel Sharon "indirectly responsible" for the massacre. It recommended that Sharon resign as defense minister, which he did.

A few days after his resignation, an article appeared in

Sharon was held partly responsible for a 1982 massacre of Palestinians in the refugee camp of Sabra. Sharon resigned his office as defense minister over the incident.

Time magazine. The article stated that Sharon had visited the Gemayel family after Bashir was assassinated. He told the family that the IDF was going into West Beirut "and that he expected the Christian forces to go into the Palestinian refugee camps. Sharon also reportedly discussed with the Gemayels the need for the Phalangists to take revenge for the assassination of Bashir. . . ."

Sharon was outraged. He sued *Time* for libel. That is, he accused the magazine of damaging his reputation by reporting something that was not true. A federal jury in Manhattan disagreed and said the article did not libel Sharon.

Sharon's role in the Lebanese massacre had hurt his standing among the people of Israel. He had also failed to create a long-lasting alliance between Lebanon and Israel to protect Israel's northern border. More than 600 IDF soldiers had been killed in the war, and Israeli public opinion was opposed to continuing the conflict. In 1983, a peace agreement was signed between Israel and Lebanon. The IDF agreed to leave Beirut, retreat, and take up a position near the Israeli border. Syria was also expected to withdraw from Lebanon. The Syrians, however, remained on Lebanese territory. Nevertheless, Israel decided to leave Beirut and reposition its soldiers southward. Syria took control of most of the country.

Battling the Palestinians

L ate in the summer of 1983, Prime Minister Menachem Begin decided to resign as head of the Israeli government. He seemed exhausted by the job. Perhaps he was also worn out from directing the war in Lebanon. Many Israelis were opposed to the war, and support for the Likud Party was declining. Begin was succeeded by Yitzhak Shamir. Sixty-eight years old, Shamir had lost his family during the Holocaust—the murder of 6 million Jews by the Nazis during World War II. Like Begin, he had later fought in the war of Israeli independence.

A year after Shamir became prime minister, another Israeli election was held. This time the votes for Likud and Labor were so close that they formed a coalition government, sharing power. Labor leader Shimon Peres served as prime minister from 1984 to 1986, while Shamir agreed to serve as leader of the government

Because neither party had a clear majority of votes, the Likud and Labor parties formed a coalition government in 1984. In this photograph, Yitzhak Shamir (second from left) and Shimon Peres (right) are seen signing the document formalizing the coalition agreement.

from 1986 to 1988. Ariel Sharon became the minister of trade and industry in the new administration. Prime Minister Peres withdrew many of the Israeli troops from Lebanon. Sharon, however, believed the decision was a tremendous mistake. He was convinced that the IDF should remain in Lebanon as the front line of defense against Palestinian terrorists.

Peres also tried to deal with the Palestinian situation in Gaza and the West Bank. Terrorists were continuing to strike

Israel from these areas. Peres believed that the West Bank and Gaza should become part of Jordan. However, the IDF would retain a military presence in the area to protect the Israeli borders. Sharon and the other Likud members of the government opposed Peres's position. They believed that Israel should annex the West Bank and Gaza, making them a permanent part of the state. Sharon wanted to establish military settlements in these areas and push out the Palestinians.

Peres initiated meetings with King Hussein of Jordan to discuss the future of the Palestinians. The prime minister also wanted to secure a peace agreement with the Jordanian king to protect Israel's eastern borders. King Hussein felt that he could not negotiate for the Palestinians without the agreement of the PLO, which was regarded by other Arab states as the representative of the Palestinians. Although he did not entirely trust Yasir Arafat, the king agreed with the PLO leader on a common approach to talks with the Israelis. They decided that the Palestinians would be given some form of self-government within the state of Jordan. However, Arafat had to agree to end his warfare against Israel. He also had to agree to United Nations Resolution 242. Passed in 1967, it called on every leader in the Middle East to respect the existence of every state there. This meant that the PLO, which had pledged itself to destroying the state of Israel, must change its policy.

While talks were going on between Arafat and Hussein, violence in the Middle East continued. Palestinian terrorists attacked Israel from Jordan. Some of Arafat's closest associates also killed three Israeli agents in Cyprus — an island nation in the Mediterranean. In retaliation, the Israelis launched an air attack against the PLO headquarters in Tunis, the capital of Tunisia. Israel's jets struck on October 1, 1985, killing many PLO terrorists.

However, the Israeli raid did not stop Peres's meetings with King Hussein. Later in October, the Israeli prime minister announced that he was going to work for a peace agreement with Jordan. King Hussein was concerned that PLO terrorists were increasing their attacks on Israel from inside Jordan. He decided to end his efforts to work with Arafat to achieve a peace treaty that included the PLO. Hussein also told the PLO to leave Amman, the capital of Jordan, where some of its leaders were living.

Before Peres could finish his work, Yitzhak Shamir became prime minister in 1986. Peres, meanwhile, began to serve as foreign minister in the Israeli government. He continued to meet with King Hussein. On one visit, in April 1987, Peres flew to London for a conference with the king. Peres was wearing a false wig so no one would recognize him. He wanted to keep the meetings with Jordan a secret, because some Israeli leaders were opposed to any agreements with the king that might eventually involve the Palestinians. Peres and King Hussein agreed that there should be a meeting of all the states concerned about the future of the Palestinians. These included Syria and Lebanon as well as a joint group of Jordanians and Palestinians.

However, Prime Minister Shamir and the other Likud ministers, including Sharon, opposed any conference that included the Palestinians. As Shamir put it: "It was always Peres's position that we must make an agreement with King Hussein . . . and give up a large piece of Judea and Samaria [the West Bank] to make peace. I was against this."

While these disagreements continued in the Israeli government, another event occurred in the Gaza Strip that would change the entire situation in the Middle East. On December 8, 1987, an Israeli military vehicle accidentally hit a car that held four young Palestinian workers and killed them. Many Palestinians were outraged. They thought the car had been struck deliberately. Large crowds of Palestinians attended the young men's funerals, which the IDF guarded to prevent trouble. Violence occurred anyway. One teenager aimed a rock at an Israeli soldier, who shot and killed him in retaliation. When news of the killing reached Palestinians throughout Gaza, they started to riot.

The *intifada,* or uprising, had begun. This was not a series of limited terrorist attacks. Suddenly, the entire Palestinian population became involved in the uprising. Rocks were being hurled at Israeli soldiers in Gaza by men, women, and children. As one high military official, deputy chief of staff Ehud Barak, explained:

> It was clear that this uprising was on a new scale, and that these people were not "terrorists" but the population itself. There was a real threat that they might overwhelm Israeli soldiers, who were there in very small numbers. If they did, this would leave the soldiers with only two possibilities: to run away, or to shoot. Both possibilities were bad. . . . We were not technically prepared to deal with a violent popular riot on this scale.

The Israeli government was divided over how to respond. Foreign Minister Peres believed that Israel should remove its settlements in Gaza and leave the area entirely to the Palestinians, but continue to govern Gaza. Shamir and Sharon disagreed. They were opposed to giving up any settlements or any control in Gaza. Defense Minister Yitzhak Rabin agreed that the IDF should take immediate action. He reportedly called on the military to "break their bones," or use force against the Palestinians. The IDF responded. Many Palestinians were arrested. Schools were closed. Curfews were clamped on Palestinian settlements. None of these actions, however, stopped the intifada. It continued, and young Israeli soldiers in the IDF were not trained to deal with a rebellion.

In Tunis, the PLO leadership had not expected a mass uprising of the Palestinian people. To retain its leadership of Palestinian affairs, the PLO began to direct the intifada. In charge of the operation was Abu Jihad. He hoped that by increasing the size of the uprising not only in Gaza but in the West Bank, the Palestinians might begin to push out the Israelis. Abu Jihad also unleashed new terrorist attacks against Israel.

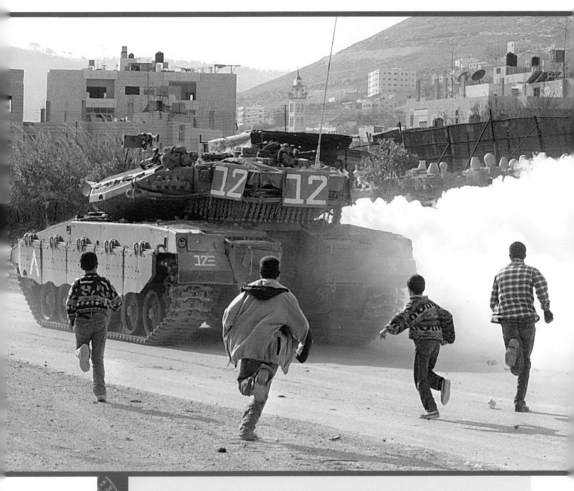

After beginning their intifada, Palestinians engaged in many forms of violence against Israel. Here, young Palestinians throw stones at a passing Israeli tank.

The Shamir government decided to strike PLO headquarters in Tunis once again. The main purpose of the mission was to kill Abu Jihad as a signal to the Palestinians that Israel would not give up its position in Gaza or the West Bank. A sneak attack was ordered on Abu Jihad's home on the night of April 15, 1988. Israeli commandos broke in, waking up Abu Jihad's wife. As she later said: "The first thing I saw was three masked men with machine guns. My husband brushed me aside, and the first of the men opened fire on him. He was wounded in the arm and heart. He turned around and fell to the ground. Then four of them, as they started running down the stairs to leave the house, shot him in rotation."

Abu Jihad's death, however, did not bring an end to the intifada. As Israel continued to battle the Palestinians, pressure began to build on the Shamir government from the United States. President Ronald Reagan became increasingly concerned that he would not be able to support the Israelis if they continued their crackdown on Palestinian civilians. Reagan, who had been a strong supporter of Israel, began to shift some of his support to the Palestinians and the PLO.

Meanwhile, Yasir Arafat recognized that the PLO had to take stronger action. The intifada, he feared, might show the Palestinians that they could drive out the Israelis without the PLO. Indeed, the uprising had unleashed new radical forces. One was a group called Hamas, which was carrying out terrorist activities independently of the PLO. Other Palestinians, however, believed that the PLO was still the best organization to negotiate with Israel for a Palestinian state. The only way that moderate Israelis, like Shimon Peres, would ever negotiate with the PLO, though, was for Arafat to agree to UN Resolution 242.

Late in 1988, Arafat made a public announcement that the PLO would finally accept the fact that Israel had the right to be a nation. This was the first step. The United States wanted Arafat to go even further, however. The Americans wanted him to also state that he would no longer use violence against the Israelis. Finally, Arafat made the announcement that the PLO would give up all forms of terrorism. The United States was then ready to begin discussions with the PLO. These were interrupted, though, by a terrorist attack in Tel Aviv by a group called the Palestine Liberation Front, which was part of the PLO.

That same year, there was another close election between Labor and Likud. As a result, they continued to run the government as a coalition. Shamir served as prime minister. Sharon still held his position as minister of trade and industry, while Rabin was reappointed defense minister. Shamir suggested a new peace proposal to his ministers. He wanted the Palestinians in Gaza and the West Bank to hold elections. They would select non-PLO representatives to negotiate an agreement with Israel to end the uprising and achieve some type of self-rule. Shamir refused to negotiate with the PLO.

Sharon was completely opposed to any kind of agreement. He believed that the Israeli government should continue to crack down on the Palestinians until the intifada was crushed. He was joined by several other members of the Israeli cabinet. The Labor Party leaders, on the other hand, did not support Sharon's position, and they were prepared to negotiate with the PLO.

The Labor leaders eventually resigned from the government early in 1990. Sharon, however, remained in the cabinet, becoming minister of housing. In this position, he began to construct 1,300 new homes on the West Bank—in line with his policy that the Israelis should continue to occupy the West Bank and not give up any territory to the Palestinians.

Two events, however, changed the situation in the Middle East. The first occurred in Moscow, the capital of the Soviet Union. The strength of the Soviet Union was in decline. President Mikhail Gorbachev had reduced the power of the Communist Party and held free elections for members of a parliament. In 1991, most of the republics that made up the Soviet Union declared their independence. As a result, the Soviet Union lost the economic and military power to assist its allies. Among them were Arab states like Syria. Without the kind of military support the Soviets had provided, the Syrians were more eager to achieve some type of peace agreement with Israel.

Sharon took a hard stance against giving any additional territory to Palestinians, who grew extremely angry when he encouraged Israeli citizens to continue to build developments, like this one on the West Bank.

The other event that occurred about the same time was the Persian Gulf War. In 1990, Saddam Hussein, the Iraqi dictator, invaded Kuwait to take control of its oil fields. In response, the United States put together a coalition to drive the Iraqis out of Kuwait. The military campaign, called Operation Desert Storm, was completely successful. Although many Arab leaders did not support Iraq, King Hussein and Yasir Arafat were among those who did. After Iraq's defeat, Hussein and Arafat were eager to improve their relations with the United States. As a result, they were willing to agree to an American proposal for a conference to discuss the Palestinian problem. Arafat was even prepared to let the Palestinians be represented by non-PLO delegates. He fully expected, however, to secretly advise them on what they should propose at the conference.

The Israeli government was not eager for the conference.

Sharon was continuing to build new houses on the West Bank. This angered the United States, whose leaders believed that new settlements would undermine the peace process. Israel depended on American financial aid, which was being used not only to build the settlements but also to find jobs for Jewish immigrants coming to Israel from Europe. American President George H.W. Bush, however, made it clear that the aid would stop unless Shamir agreed to a peace conference.

This was enough to bring the Israelis, the Palestinians, and the Arab states together for talks in Madrid, Spain, beginning in October 1991.

The Quest
for Peace

After more than 40 years of warfare, peace would not come easily. Prime Minister Shamir insisted that Syria and Jordan accept United Nations Resolution 242, recognizing the state of Israel. The Syrians and Jordanians wanted Israel to give up the West Bank, Gaza, and the Golan Heights. The Palestinians also expected to receive some land to use to eventually establish a new state. But Shamir had no intention of giving up any of the territory that Israel had conquered during the 1967 war. The prime minister and his supporters, including Ariel Sharon, were convinced that this land was essential for Israel to defend itself against possible attack by the Arabs.

As a result, the meetings in Madrid accomplished very little. Meanwhile, Israel was preparing to hold another national election. The Labor Party, led by Yitzhak Rabin, promised to achieve some

Another major step in the peace process was taken in 1993, when Israeli Prime Minister Yitzhak Rabin (left) and PLO Chairman Yasir Arafat (right) signed a peace accord.

kind of peace agreement with the Palestinians. Rabin also wanted to stop building Jewish settlements on the West Bank. In June 1992, Labor won a tremendous victory, sweeping the Likud Party from office. The need for a peace agreement became even more important as incidents between Israel and the Palestinians increased. Late in 1992, an Israeli border guard was killed. Rabin responded by rounding up more than 400 members of Hamas and forcing them to leave Israel and go to Lebanon. Rabin also assaulted Hamas bases in Lebanon during 1993, after terrorist attacks were made on Israel.

While these incidents were occurring, secret peace talks were under way. Israeli and PLO representatives were meeting in Oslo, Norway. After lengthy discussions, the negotiators finally agreed to a Declaration of Principles on Interim Self-Government Arrangements. The declaration was also known as Oslo I. Israel recognized the PLO as the legitimate representative of the Palestinians. In turn, the PLO recognized the right of Israel to be a state. The negotiators also agreed that the Palestinians should begin to take control of much of Gaza and areas on the West Bank. The agreement was formally signed by Arafat and Rabin in Washington, D.C., on September 13, 1993. U.S. President Bill Clinton emphasized the importance of the agreement in the peace process. One historian has called it among "the most momentous events in the history of the Middle East in the twentieth century."

Sharon, who was no longer a member of the government, was highly critical of the Oslo agreement. He accused Rabin of being a "traitor" to the Israeli people and said that Likud would never have signed such an agreement. Binyamin Netanyahu, who had become the new leader of the Likud Party, said that Rabin was helping Arafat set up a "Palestinian terrorist state." Some Palestinians, such as those in Hamas, criticized Arafat for not demanding more from the Israelis. They wanted to see the immediate establishment of a Palestinian state in Gaza and the West Bank.

Nevertheless, negotiations between the Israelis and the Palestinians continued. In May 1994, they agreed in Cairo for the PLO to take control of towns in the Gaza Strip from the IDF. Arafat moved to Gaza, where he set up the Palestinian capital. In September 1995, Arafat and Rabin signed another agreement, known as Oslo II. The IDF prepared to leave important towns on the West Bank and turn them over to the Palestinians. These included Jenin and Nablus in the north, Ramallah and Jericho in the center, and Bethlehem and Hebron in the south. This was about 4 percent of the West Bank. The Israelis retained control of some areas of the West Bank to protect their settlers. Israel and the Palestinians shared power in other areas, about one-third of the West Bank. In Gaza, the Palestinians governed about 65 percent of the territory, while the IDF remained in the rest, where the Israeli settlements were located.

Not only had Rabin achieved a breakthrough agreement with the Palestinians, but he also made peace with Jordan. Both King Hussein and Rabin wanted to end the years of warfare between their two nations. In November 1995, Rabin spoke to a large peace rally in Tel Aviv. "I was a soldier for 27 years," he told the crowd. "I fought so long as there was no prospect of peace. I believe that there is now a chance for peace, a great chance, which must be seized."

After finishing his speech, Rabin left the rally and went to his car. Suddenly, he was approached by a lone gunman named Yigal Amir, a man who was opposed to the peace agreements with the Palestinians. Amir took out a pistol and shot Rabin three times. The 73-year-old prime minister died a short time later. Israel was stunned. Yasir Arafat said, "I have lost a friend. This is a great loss to the cause of peace and to me personally." The Likud, which had strongly opposed the Oslo agreements, lost popularity in Israel. Many Israelis, who mourned the loss of Rabin, wanted to continue the peace process as a tribute to their dead leader.

The Labor Party selected Shimon Peres to replace Rabin. Peres had served as foreign minister in the Rabin administration. He was committed to continuing the peace efforts. However, the situation remained dangerous. Radical groups like Hamas still opposed peace. Early in 1996, Peres authorized the assassination of a Hamas leader, Yahya Ayyash, who had spearheaded terrorist attacks in Israel. When a cell phone Ayyash was using blew up and killed him, Hamas immediately retaliated. Terrorist attacks increased, and Peres seemed incapable of stopping them. Suddenly, the Likud Party, which had always supported a hard line against the Palestinians, began to gain new support in Israel.

Meanwhile, the Hamas attacks continued. From its bases in southern Lebanon, Hamas launched rockets against Israeli settlements in the Galilee. Finally, the Peres government launched an attack on Lebanon, aimed at destroying the Hamas positions there. Called Operation Grapes of Wrath, the Israeli assault was aimed at Beirut and the Bekaa Valley. By mistake, Israeli shells hit a refugee camp maintained by the United Nations, killing more than 100 people. Peres was criticized throughout the Middle East. The United States finally stepped in and pressured Israel to stop the war.

In the Israeli elections of May 1996, many voters showed that they had lost confidence in Peres. He was narrowly defeated by Binyamin Netanyahu, who became the new prime minister. Netanyahu was only 46 years old, but he had much experience in government. During the 1980s, he served as a diplomat in Washington and later as Israeli representative to the United Nations. He had also been deputy foreign minister in Yitzhak Shamir's administration. During the 1990s, he wrote a book, *A Place Among Nations*. In it, he criticized the Arab states for constantly using violence and warned against making any agreements with them. Netanyahu was highly critical of the Oslo agreements.

The new prime minister invited Ariel Sharon to become a member of his administration and serve as minister of national infrastructure. Sharon's department was in charge of Israeli settlements on the West Bank. Both he and Netanyahu agreed that these settlements should continue. They also strongly opposed any new Palestinian state. Finally, Sharon and

Netanyahu believed that Israel should remain in complete control of Jerusalem. The Palestinians, however, demanded to have East Jerusalem as their capital.

The Oslo agreements had called for Israel to continue to hand over more territory to the Palestinians. The new Likud government made no effort to continue this process, however. In September, Netanyahu took a step that angered many Palestinians. He opened up a tunnel to give Israelis another way to get to the Western Wall in East Jerusalem. This wall, which was part of an ancient Jewish temple, is an important religious site for Jews. Part of the temple, though, is the site of the Dome of the Rock. This mosque (a Muslim religious building used for worship) is sacred to Arabs. It is believed to be the place where Muhammad, who founded Islam in the seventh century, left Earth and ascended into heaven. The Palestinians living in East Jerusalem were outraged. They feared that the tunnel might weaken the foundations of the Dome of the Rock. The Palestinians also believed that the Israelis were trying to tighten their control of East Jerusalem, instead of discussing the possibility that it might become the new Palestinian capital.

Violence broke out among the Palestinians on the West Bank and in the Gaza Strip. To reduce the violence, the Clinton administration pressured Netanyahu to continue with the Oslo peace process. On January 15, 1997, Israel signed the Hebron Protocol. Under this agreement, Netanyahu gave up control of most of Hebron, which the Israelis were supposed to hand over as part of the Oslo agreement. The IDF stayed in part of the city to protect Israeli settlers there. Some members of the Likud, including Sharon, opposed the agreement. As Sharon put it, the prime minister was "a dangerous man for the state of Israel." Sharon was convinced that Netanyahu had given away too much land to the Palestinians.

Nevertheless, pressure on Netanyahu continued from the United States. In 1998, he agreed to meet Arafat at a peace

Palestinians protest tunnel

Palestinians in Jerusalem and the West Bank protested the opening of a 484-meter-long tunnel that links the Western Wall, Judaism's holiest site, with the Via Dolorosa, the street where Jesus is believed to have walked on the way to his crucifixion.

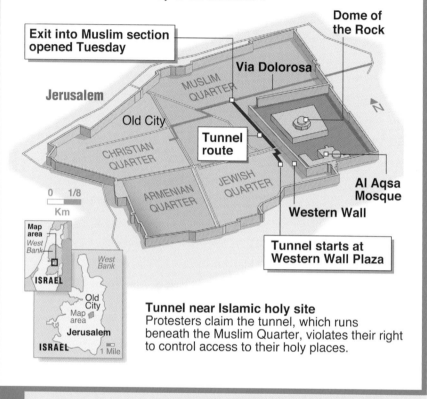

Exit into Muslim section opened Tuesday

Dome of the Rock

Via Dolorosa

Jerusalem

MUSLIM QUARTER

Old City

CHRISTIAN QUARTER

Tunnel route

ARMENIAN QUARTER

JEWISH QUARTER

Al Aqsa Mosque

Western Wall

0   1/8
Km

Map area
West Bank

ISRAEL
West Bank

Old City
Map area
Jerusalem
ISRAEL
1 Mile

Tunnel starts at Western Wall Plaza

Tunnel near Islamic holy site
Protesters claim the tunnel, which runs beneath the Muslim Quarter, violates their right to control access to their holy places.

Palestinians fiercely opposed a tunnel Israel built as a new route to the Western Wall of Jerusalem. As Muslims, the Palestinians feared the tunnel would cause harm to the Dome of the Rock, a sacred site.

conference at the Wye River Plantation in Maryland, near Washington, D.C. Netanyahu was accompanied by Sharon, who was his new foreign minister. He had given Sharon this powerful cabinet post to satisfy members of the Likud who supported Sharon's hard-line position against the Palestinians.

On October 23, 1998, the Palestinians and Israelis came to an agreement at Wye. Called the Wye River Memorandum, it called on Israel to hand over 40 percent of the West Bank to the Palestinians during the next three months. In return, Arafat said that he would try to deal with terrorism from extreme Palestinian groups, like Hamas.

Some members of the Likud Party as well as other political groups in Israel opposed the agreement. Sharon supported it, though. "We participated in very tough negotiations, perhaps the most difficult ever," he said. "I believe we achieved the best results possible." Tensions still ran high over Jerusalem, however. Arafat announced that Palestinians would use violence if Israel tried to prevent them from worshiping at the mosques there. Netanyahu, in turn, announced that he would not give in on any attempt to divide Jerusalem. Meanwhile, Sharon was urging Israeli settlers to take over more land on the West Bank. "Everyone should take action, should run, should grab more hills," he said. "We'll expand the area. Whatever is seized will be ours. Whatever isn't seized will end up in their hands."

More settlers began to set up homes on the West Bank. At the same time, however, Israel also began to withdraw from small amounts of territory mentioned in the Wye agreement. Nevertheless, Netanyahu found himself losing support among the Likud. Many other Israelis, however, believed that the peace process had not gone far enough. In 1999, Barak formed the One Israel Party from Labor and other factions; in May, his party won the next election in 1999, and he took over the government. Ariel Sharon gave up his position as foreign minister.

After the election, Barak promised to "put an end to the suffering of the Palestinian people" by broadening the peace efforts. On September 4, 1999, Barak and Arafat signed the Sharm al-Sheikh Agreement, calling for Israel to hand over more territory on the West Bank to the Palestinians. In addition, Israel agreed to guarantee safe passage for Palestinians between the Gaza Strip and the West Bank. Sharon opposed the agreement and, in a speech to the Knesset, said that Barak had received nothing in return for his concessions to the Palestinians. Sharon spoke as the new leader of the Likud Party. He had won the leadership position after the elections in 1999.

While Sharon's political power was increasing, he suffered a grave personal loss. On March 25, 2000, his wife, Lily, died of cancer. They had been married for more than 35 years. Lily had always been a strong supporter of Sharon's political career. At the funeral service, Sharon said: "Until today I never acted without you. From now on it will be without you. It will not be easy. But I will continue to go on the path in which both of us believed." She was buried at the Sharon farm in the Negev.

In July 2000, President Bill Clinton, Barak, and Arafat met at Camp David in an attempt to create a broad peace agreement. After many hours of negotiations, though, the talks were unsuccessful. Arafat wanted complete control of East Jerusalem, as well as all of the West Bank and Gaza Strip. It was too much for Barak to give up. After returning to Israel, Barak found that his political support was rapidly disappearing. Since his peace efforts had failed, many voters lost confidence in his ability to continue to run Israel.

Instead, support was gradually increasing for Ariel Sharon to become prime minister. On September 28, Sharon decided to visit the Temple Mount in East Jerusalem. This site is sacred to both Arabs and Jews. Many Palestinians were angered that someone like Sharon, a Jew and a leader who had so firmly opposed any peace agreements, should visit the Temple Mount. Palestinian political leaders called the visit a "flagrant aggression against the holy places and disregard for the feelings of the Palestinian people and the Arab and Islamic nations" and said that it "would create an explosive situation in the holy city."

The peace process continued through the 1990s, as Israel and the Palestinians came to many new understandings. Here, Yasir Arafat (left) and Israeli Prime Minister Ehud Barak (right) hold up a box containing a copy of the Muslim Koran and Jewish Bible, a gift from Barak to Arafat.

They were right. After Sharon's visit, violence broke out in East Jerusalem. By the following day, the West Bank and Gaza were also scenes of bloody confrontations between young Palestinians and the IDF. It was the beginning of a new intifada. By the beginning of October, more than 80 people had died. Barak and Arafat seemed unable to stop the bloodshed. The death toll rose to more than 100 by the middle of the month.

Some Israelis held Sharon responsible for triggering the new intifada, by doing something that provoked such a reaction. They also believed, however, that Barak's peace efforts had led to nothing. He had been willing to give up large amounts of

Insulted by Sharon's visit to the Muslim sacred site at Temple Mount, Palestinians once again began an intifada of violence against Israel.

territory to the Palestinians, but Arafat had still not been satisfied. The United Nations, however, disagreed. The UN General Assembly said that it was Sharon's trip to the Temple Mount alone that had led to the deaths in the intifada.

Sharon paid no attention to the United Nations. He accused the Palestinians of looking for any reason to start an uprising. As the unrest continued, more people died. By the middle of November, 230 people had died and 8,000 had been injured in clashes between the IDF and the Palestinians.

In December 2000, Barak called for new elections. He wanted to find out if the Israeli people would support him in the future or vote instead for the Likud. His opponent for prime minister would be Sharon.

Prime Minister

T
hroughout his political career, Ariel Sharon had always taken
a strong position on negotiations with the Palestinians. Now
many Israeli voters believed that this was the only way to deal
with them. Prime Minister Barak's efforts to negotiate peace had
been a failure. Sharon said during the election campaign that he
would not give up any of the Jewish settlements in Gaza or the West
Bank. He also promised that all of Jerusalem would remain part of
Israel. Nevertheless, Sharon indicated that he was prepared to deal
with Yasir Arafat. "As a Jew," he said, "I know it is not easy to be a
Palestinian. We have to take steps to make the Palestinians' lives
easier." Referring to the land that had been given to the Palestinian
Authority, he added: "We are the only nation in the world ready to
give up our cradle, part of our history, to reach peace."

The election returns on February 6, 2001, gave Sharon an

Many Israeli citizens, especially those who have faced the danger of Palestinian violence, supported Sharon because of his tough stance on Palestine and his refusal to give in to demands in the form of violence.

impressive victory over Barak. Although Israelis wanted peace, they felt that only Sharon's firm position toward the Palestinians could achieve it. Barak immediately gave up his position as head of the Labor Party and was succeeded by Shimon Peres. Meanwhile, violence continued between Israel and the Palestinians. In the Gaza Strip, the IDF killed one of Arafat's closest advisors. He was accused of plotting terrorist acts against Israel. On February 14, a Palestinian bus driver ran into a crowd of pedestrians in Tel Aviv and killed eight of them. He was later shot by the police while driving away. In the Gaza Strip, the IDF battled armed Palestinians for six hours. They were protesting Israeli occupation in parts of Gaza.

In early March, Sharon formed a coalition government that included members of the Likud and Labor parties. Shimon

Peres became foreign minister, while Yitzhak Rabin's daughter, Dalia Rabin-Pelossof, was named deputy defense minister. Sharon addressed the Knesset, saying that he was prepared to have peace talks with Arafat if he made an effort to stop the violence. Sharon insisted that there should be at least ten days without a violent act before any discussions could begin. Many Arabs believed, however, that Sharon would never negotiate with the Palestinians. As one newspaper put it: "By electing Sharon and sacrificing Barak, Israelis have voted against peace."

Since the violence did not stop, Sharon began to take other actions against the Palestinians. In March, the IDF started digging large trenches around several towns on the West Bank. These included Ramallah and Jericho, considered centers of terrorist activity. The trenches were designed to cut off the Palestinians there from the rest of the West Bank. But the trenches also prevented many Palestinians from traveling to jobs in nearby areas. Without work, these Palestinians and their families fell on hard times. Also in March, Sharon went to Washington, where he was warmly welcomed by President George W. Bush. Nevertheless, the Bush administration asked him to let Palestinians travel between their jobs and their homes so they could continue to support their families.

Late in March, more violence occurred. A young Jewish girl was killed in Hebron on the West Bank by Palestinians living in another part of the town. Jewish settlers reacted immediately and began to burn part of the Palestinian section. A day later, bombs were set off in Jerusalem by the Islamic Jihad terrorist group, injuring 30 people. Later in March, a suicide bomber killed several Jewish schoolchildren at a bus stop in Qalqilya on the West Bank. Sharon retaliated against Arafat, whom he blamed for not controlling the violence. He sent Israeli helicopters in a missile attack against Palestinian government buildings in Ramallah and Gaza. Another strike came in April after Palestinian attacks on Israeli settlements in Gaza.

While Sharon was striking out at the Palestinians, he

was also trying to pursue talks with Arafat. One of his closest political advisors was his son, Omri. He was carrying on a series of meetings with Arafat, trying to reach an agreement. These meetings were criticized by some members of Sharon's coalition. They believed that no talks should occur unless Arafat ended the violence. Some political experts, however, wondered if Arafat actually could control it. They believed that more radical Palestinian groups might be operating independently of Arafat, even though he was head of the Palestinian Authority. These groups had grown frustrated with peace efforts and had become convinced that only violence could force the Israelis out of the West Bank and Gaza.

However, Palestinian terrorism only brought an increased level of violence from Israel. In mid-April, the IDF invaded Gaza. Many Palestinians there live in refugee camps. Their homes and small farms were struck by Israeli soldiers searching for armed terrorists. The Israeli attacks increased after artillery fire from the Palestinian town of Beit Hanoun hit a Jewish settlement. The IDF occupied territory that was supposed to be controlled by the Palestinian Authority. Another battle erupted between the IDF and Palestinians on the West Bank near Bethlehem.

However, pressure was increasing on Sharon to cut down the level of violence. The United States wanted the prime minister to consider discussions with Arafat. In addition, Jordan and Egypt urged the Israeli government to allow the Palestinians in the West Bank towns to travel freely. They also wanted Israel to stop building Jewish settlements. Sharon responded by saying that Palestinian terrorism must stop before he would negotiate. The violence, which had begun in the fall of 2000, had already resulted in the deaths of more than 70 Israelis and 400 Palestinians.

In May, a report on Israeli-Palestinian peace was issued by an American commission headed by former Democratic Senator George Mitchell. The Mitchell report called on Sharon to let the Palestinians on the West Bank travel to their jobs and not to

Despite all the progress made in the Arab-Israeli conflict over the past few decades, much remains to be done. The violence continues and even seems to be escalating. Here, Palestinians shout virulent anti-Israel slogans as they carry the body of a teenager who was killed by Israeli troops in a gun battle within Palestinian territory.

increase Jewish settlements. Sharon had always been committed to the growth of Israeli settlements in areas he considered part of the traditional Jewish lands. He refused to change his position to achieve peace. As he put it, "we do not have to pay in order not to get killed. It's very simple. We will not pay protection money." The Israelis who established these settlements had always been among his strongest supporters.

Neither Israel nor the Palestinians would change their positions. Consequently, there was no end to the violence. In May, after a suicide bomber killed six Israelis at a shopping mall, Sharon unleashed a furious attack against the Palestinian Authority. Israeli jets hit Palestinian government positions on the West Bank and Gaza. In the meantime, Sharon continued to feel pressure from the United States to take the first steps toward peace. After the Israeli air assault, he finally agreed to a cease-fire.

During May and June 2001, Palestinian terrorist attacks and suicide bombings continued. One of these bombings occurred at the Dolphinarium, a dance club in Tel Aviv. Twenty-one young Israelis were killed and 90 people were wounded. Some of Sharon's political allies wanted him to retaliate against the Palestinian Authority. Nevertheless, he continued to maintain the cease-fire. In June, Israel and the Palestinian Authority agreed to a plan submitted by George Tenet, head of the U.S. Central Intelligence Agency (CIA). It called on Sharon to stop isolating Palestinian towns. In return, Arafat would clamp down on the violence. However, the prime minister was criticized by some members of his party, who said that the Tenet plan would not provide enough protection to Israeli settlers on the West Bank.

In June, Sharon went back to Washington. There, he said: "The cycle of violence must be broken." Nevertheless, the terrorist attacks continued. Finally, in August, Sharon ended the cease-fire and retaliated. He sent the IDF into Beit Jala, a town on the West Bank that was a center of radical Palestinians. Still, the suicide bombings by Palestinians continued in September.

Once again, the Israeli government agreed to a cease-fire, but it was followed by more battles between the IDF and Palestinians as well as a car bombing in Jerusalem. It seemed to be an endless cycle—one incident, followed by a response, followed by still another violent response.

Ariel Sharon had spent most of his life in the army or in politics, defending the state of Israel and battling against the Palestinians. Once he had finally achieved the position of prime minister, he could find no solution to the violence that had engulfed the area for decades. Tragically, the violent course of events seemed likely to continue for Arabs and Jews, with no end in sight.

1928 Ariel Sharon is born in Palestine.

1936 Arabs revolt against Jews in Palestine.

1948 Israel becomes a state.

1953 Sharon marries Margalit Zimmerman; organizes Commando Unit 101.

1956 Israel fights in the Suez War against Egypt.

1962 Sharon's wife is killed; he remarries the following year.

1967 Israel wins Six-Day War against Arabs, triples size of the country.

1973 Israel battles Egypt and Syria in Yom Kippur War.

1977 Likud wins general election; Sharon joins Likud cabinet as minister of agriculture.

1979 Peace agreement is reached between Israel and Egypt.

1982 Israel invades Lebanon under Sharon's direction as defense minister.

1984 Sharon becomes minister of trade and industry.

1987 Palestinian intifada begins.

1993 Oslo agreement is signed.

1996 Sharon becomes minister of national infrastructure.

1999 Sharon becomes leader of Likud Party.

2000 New intifada begins; Sharon's wife dies.

2001 Sharon is elected prime minister.

2003 Sharon is reelected prime minister.

Benziman, Yuzi. *Sharon: An Israeli Caesar.* New York: Adama Books, 1985.

Bregman, Ahron, and Jihan El-Tahri. *The Fifty Years' War: Israel and the Arabs.* New York: TV Books, 1998.

La Guardia, Anton. *War Without End: Israelis, Palestinians and the Struggle for a Promised Land.* New York: St. Martin's Press, 2001.

Miller, Anita, et al. *Sharon: Israel's Warrior-Politician.* Chicago: Academy Chicago Publishers, 2002.

Sharon, Ariel. *Warrior: An Autobiography.* New York: Simon and Schuster, 1989.

Shlaim, Avi. *The Iron Wall: Israel and the Arab World.* New York: W.W. Norton, 2000.

Articles

Bennet, James. "Puzzle for Israel: What Does Sharon Want?" *The New York Times,* January 30, 2003.

Eisenberg, Daniel, et al. "Arafat's Dance of Death," *Time,* December 24, 2001.

Ephron, Dan, and Joanna Chen. "A Peace Deal—Or a Partition." *Newsweek,* December 2, 2002.

Shikaki, Khalil. "Palestinians Divided." *Foreign Affairs,* January/February 2002.

Rees, Matt, et al. "The Pressure on Sharon," *Time,* September 10, 2001.

Abu Agheila, 43
Afula, 19
Al-Aksa Martyrs Brigade, 23
Al Qaeda, 17
Amir, Yigal, 79
Annex Research, 14
Arabs
    in Palestine, 28, 29, 31
    and revolts against Jews in
        Palestine, 29, 30, 31-32
    and war at creation of state of
        Israel, 32-33
    and war at partition of Palestine,
        31-32
Arafat, Yasir
    and Israeli attacks against head-
        quarters, 19, 21, 23-24
    and negotiations with Israel,
        81-84, 93
    and Oslo agreements, 78
    and Palestinian Authority, 15, 18,
        91
    and Palestinian state, 15, 21
    and Palestinian violence, 19-21,
        23, 83
    and PLO, 46, 68, 72
    as prisoner in Ramallah, 21
    and Rabin's assassination, 79
    and released as prisoner in
        Ramallah, 23
    and Sharon, 15, 18, 19-21, 23-24,
        88, 90-91
    and 2000 intifada, 85
Ayyash, Yahya, 80

Barak, Ehud
    and negotiations with
        Palestinians, 88
    as prime minister, 83-84,
        85-87
    and 2000 intifada, 85
Bar-Lev, Chaim, 45, 46
Bar-Lev line, 45, 46, 51
Battle of the Roads, 31
Bedouins, 47-48

Begin, Menachim
    and control of Jerusalem, 57
    and Herut Party, 49
    and Irgun, 31
    and Likud Party, 49, 56-58, 61,
        62, 63
    and peace agreement with Egypt,
        57-59
    as prime minister, 31, 56-59
    and West Bank settlements,
        56-57, 60
Beit Hanoun, 91
Beit Jala, 93
Bekaa Valley, 80
Ben Gurion, David, 32
Bethlehem, 22, 79
Bir Addas, 32
Bush, George W.
    and negotiations between
        Israelis and Palestinians, 23
    Sharon meeting with, 21, 90,
        93

Camp David Accords, 57-59,
    84
Carter, Jimmy, 57-59
casualties, from Israeli-Palestinian
    clashes, 17, 18, 22, 85, 89, 91
Church of the Nativity (Bethlehem),
    22
Clinton, Bill, 78, 84
Commando Unit 101, 35-38

David, King, 26
Dayan, Moshe, 34, 37, 38, 40
diaspora, 26-27
Dolphinarium, 93
Dome of the Rock, 81

East Jerusalem
    and Palestinians, 81, 83
    and Sharon's visit to Temple
        Mount, 84-87
economy, and recession in Israel,
    17-18

Egypt
    and free travel for Palestinians in
        West Bank, 91
    and Nasser, 38, 42, 45, 48
    and peace agreement with Israel,
        57-59
    and Sadat, 48-49, 57-59
    Sharon's commando raids against,
        37-38
    and Six-Day War, 42-44
    and Soviet aid, 38, 46
    and Suez War, 38-39
    and terrorist attacks against Israel,
        35
    and war at creation of state of
        Israel, 32
    and Yom Kippur War, 50-53
El Arish, 43
Eshkol, Levi, 42

fedayeen, 36
France, and Suez War, 38-39

Galilee, 60, 80
Gaza City, 19
Gaza Strip
    fence separating Israel from
        settlements on, 24
    Israeli settlements in, 60
    and Palestinian Authority, 15
    Palestinian control of, 78, 79
    in Palestinian state, 21
    and safe passage for Palestinians, 84
    Sharon building settlements on, 88
    and Six-Day War, 42
    and Suez War, 39
    violence between Israelis
        and Palestinians in, 17, 18,
        35-36, 37-38, 48, 81, 89, 90,
        91, 92
    and War of Attrition, 46
Golan Heights
    and Egyptian buildup, 48
    and Six-Day War, 44
    and Yom Kippur War, 51, 53

Gonen, Shmuel, 51
Great Britain
    and control of Palestine, 28, 30-31
    and Suez War, 38-39
    and withdrawal from Palestine, 31
Gulf of Aqaba, 42

Haganah, 31
    See also Israeli Defense Forces
Haifa, 19
Hamas
    and Arafat, 20, 83
    and attacks against Israel, 17, 19,
        20, 21, 22, 80
    Israeli attacks against, 24
    and Oslo agreements, 78
    and peace efforts, 79-80
Hebrew University, 34
Hebron
    Palestinian control of, 79, 81
    violence between Israelis and
        Palestinians in, 90
Hebron Protocol, 81
Herut Party, 49
Herzl, Theodor, 28
Hussein, King, 56, 60, 79

Idris, Wafa, 21
Iraq
    and Six-Day War, 42
    and war at creation of state of
        Israel, 32
Irgun, 31
Islamic Jihad, 90
Israel
    creation of state of, 31, 32-33
    recognition of as state, 78
Israeli Defense Forces (IDF)
    and Arab terrorist attacks after
        Israeli independence, 35-38
    creation of, 32
    and Egyptian buildup, 48-49
    and guerrilla mission against
        Jordanian terrorist, 34-35
    and invasion of Lebanon, 60, 61-65

and 1987 intifada, 70
and Palestinian terrorism under
    Sharon, 19, 21-22, 23, 24, 89,
    90-93
and PLO, 46-48
Sharon in, 32-39, 41-46, 49, 50-53,
    54, 56
and Six-Day War, 42-44
and Suez War, 38-39
and 2000 intifada, 85-87
and war at creation of state of
    Israel, 32-33
and War of Attrition, 45-46
and withdrawal from Gaza and
    West Bank, 79
and Yom Kippur War, 50-53

Jenin
    Israeli attack on, 22
    Israeli's searching for terrorists
        in, 22
    Palestinian control of, 79
Jericho
    Palestinian control of, 79
    trenches around, 90
Jerusalem
    as capital of Israel, 21
    as capital of kingdom of Israel, 26
    as capital of Palestinian state, 21,
        81, 83
    Israeli control of, 80-81, 83, 88
    renamed Palestine, 26
    and Roman control, 26
    Sharon building settlements
        around, 57
    and Six-Day War, 44
    violence between Israelis and
        Palestinians in, 19, 23, 90, 93
Jews
    and immigration to Palestine,
        28, 29, 30, 31
    and kingdom of Israel, 26
    and opposition to British rule
        of Palestine, 31
    persecution of, 26-28, 29, 30

Jordan
    and free travel for Palestinians in
        West Bank, 91
    and King Hussein, 56, 60, 79
    and peace with Israel, 79
    Sharon freeing soldiers from, 34
    Sharon leading guerrilla expedition
        against terrorist in, 34-35
    and Six-Day War, 42
    and terrorist attacks against Israel,
        35
    and war at creation of state of
        Israel, 32-33
Judea, 57
    See also West Bank

Kenya, terrorism against Jews in, 17
Kern, Cyril, 14
Keussaima, and Six-Day War, 43
Kfar Malal
    clash between Arabs and Jews in,
        31-32
    Sharon's early years in, 28-30
Kibbiya, Sharon's commando raid
    on, 37
King David Hotel, and Irgun
    bombing, 31
Knesset
    Likud Party in, 12-13, 14, 54, 59
    Sharon in, 54, 56
Kuntilla, Sharon's commando raid
    on, 38

Labor Party
    and Barak, 89
    and Meier, 55
    and Mitzna, 14
    and negotiations with
        Palestinians, 83
    and Peres, 79-80, 89
    Sharon leading coalition
        against, 49
    and War of Attrition, 46
    and Yom Kippur War, 54
Latrun, 32-33

Lebanon
civil war in, 60
Hamas in, 80
Israeli invasion of, 60, 61-63
Peres's attack on, 80
PLO in, 60, 61-63
and war at creation of state of
Israel, 32
Likud Party
and Begin, 56-58, 61, 62, 63
corruption in, 13-15
formation of, 12, 49
and hard line against Palestinians,
80
in Knesset, 12-13, 14, 54, 59
and negotiations with Palestinians,
81, 83
and Netanyahu, 80-83
and Rabin's assassination, 79
and Sharon, 12-15, 56-57, 61-63,
81-83, 84

Meir, Golda, 51, 55
Mitgla Pass, 38, 40, 43
Mitzna, Amram
moshav, 28
Muslims, and rule of Palestine, 27

Nablus
Palestinian control of, 79
violence between Israelis and
Palestinians in, 22
Nakhel, and Six-Day War, 43
Nasser, Gamal Abdel, 38, 42, 45
Nazis, and persecution of Jews, 29,
30
Negev
and War of Attrition, 46
Netanya, 21
Netanyahu, Binyamin, 78
and Jerusalem, 81, 83
and negotiations with Palestinians,
81-83
as prime minister, 80-83
and tunnel to Western Wall, 81

Odeh, Abdel-Basset, 21
One Israel, 83
Operation Defense Shield, 21
Operation Grapes of Wrath, 80
Oslo agreements, 78-79, 80, 81
Ottoman Empire, 28

Palestine
Arab revolt against Jews in, 29, 30,
31-32
Arabs living in, 28, 29, 31
and British control, 28, 30, 31
and diaspora, 26-27
immigration of Jews to, 28, 29, 30,
31
and Muslim rule, 27
and Ottoman Empire, 28
partition of, 31
and return of Jews, 27
Romans renaming Jerusalem as,
26
Palestine Liberation Organization
(PLO)
and Arafat, 46, 68, 72
formation of, 46
and Israel as state, 78
and Israeli Defense Forces, 46-48
and Jordan, 46, 56, 60
and Lebanon, 60, 61-63
and negotiations with Israel, 78-79
and Sharon's attack on in Negev,
46-47
Palestinian Authority
and Arafat, 18, 91
and Israeli attack on airport of, 19
Israeli negotiations with, 93
land given to, 88
Sharon's attack on, 92-93
territories of, 15
and violence against Israel, 18
Palestinians
and control of Gaza and West
Bank, 78, 79
and East Jerusalem as capital, 81,
83

and inability to travel to jobs, 24,
90, 91
and negotiations with Israel, 80,
81-84, 85-86, 88, 89, 90, 91-93
state for, 15, 18, 21, 60
and 2000 intifada, 85-87
and United Nations, 31
and violence against Israel, 15-25,
89-94
Peres, Shimon
and attack on Lebanon, 80
as foreign minister, 90
and Hamas, 79-80
and Labor Party, 89
as prime minister, 79
pogroms, 27-28
post-action reports, 37

Qalqilya, 90

Rabin-Pelossof, Dalia, 90
Rabin, Yitzhak
assassination of, 79
as commander-in-chief, 42
and peace with Jordan, 79
as prime minister, 55-56
Rafah, 43
Ramallah
Arafat as prisoner in, 21
Arafat leaving headquarters in,
23
Israeli attacks against, 19, 21,
23-24, 80
Palestinian control of, 79
trenches around, 90
Red Sea, 42
Rome, and control of Jerusalem, 26
Russia, persecution of Jews in, 27-28

Sadat, Anwar, 48-49
and peace agreement between
Israel and Egypt, 57-59
Safi, and PLO, 46
Samaria, 57
See also West Bank

Scheinerman, Dita (sister), 28
Scheinerman, Dvora (mother), 28,
29, 30
Scheinerman, Samuil (father), 28, 29
Sharm al-Sheikh Agreement, 83-84
Sharon, Ariel
as agriculture minister, 56-57
and Arab revolt against Jews in
Palestine, 31-32
and Arafat, 15, 18, 19-21, 23-24,
88, 90-91
and "Arik" as nickname, 12
and attack on Iraq, 61
and attacks against PLO, 46-48
and battle injury, 32-33
birth of, 28
childhood of, 28-30
children of, 40, 45, 49, 91
and coalition government, 12,
89-90
and Commando Unit 101, 35-38
and corruption, 13-15
as defense minister, 12, 61-63
education of, 29-30, 34, 40
family of, 28-29, 30
as farmer in Negev, 49
as foreign minister, 12, 82-83
and formation of Likud Party, 49
and formation of Shlomzion
Party, 56
and freeing Israeli soldiers from
Jordanians, 34
and guerrilla expedition against
Jordanian terrorist, 34-35
in Haganah, 31-32
and Hebron Protocol, 81
and infantry training school, 40
and invasion of Lebanon, 60, 61-65
and Israel becoming a state, 32-33
in Israeli Defense Forces, 32-39,
41-46, 49, 50-53, 54, 56
in Knesset, 54, 56
and Lebanese massacre, 63-65
and Likud Party, 12-15, 56-57, 61-63,
81-83, 84

as major general, 42
and malaria, 34
and marriages. *See* Sharon, Lily
	Zimmerman; Sharon, Margalit
	Zimmerman
and meetings with Bush, 21, 23, 93
as minister of housing, 73
as minister of trade and industry,
	67, 73
and name change, 28
and negotiations with Palestinians,
	76, 81-83, 84, 88, 89, 90, 91-93
and Northern Command, 41-42
and Operation Defense Shield, 21
and Oslo agreements, 78
and Palestinian Authority, 18
and Palestinian state, 21
and Palestinian violence, 15-25,
	89-94
and peace agreement between
	Egypt and Israel, 58-59
personality of, 29-30
and position against Palestinians,
	15-25
as prime minister, 12, 13-14, 18,
	84, 88-94
and re-election as prime minister,
	12-15, 24
and settlements around Jerusalem,
	57
and Sharm al-Sheikh agreement,
	84
and Shehada's death, 24
and Six-Day War, 42-44, 46
and Southern Command, 46
and Suez War, 38-39, 40
and training for Israeli Defense
	Forces, 44-45
and visit to Temple Mount, 84-87
and War of Attrition, 45-46
and West Bank settlements, 15,
	56-57, 59, 60, 68, 73, 75, 80, 83,
	90-91
and withdrawal of troops from
	Lebanon, 67

and Wye River Memorandum,
	83
and Yom Kippur War, 50-53
and Zeevi's assassination, 18
Sharon, Gilad (son), 4
Sharon, Gur (son), 40, 45
Sharon, Lily Zimmerman (second
	wife), 40-41, 45, 84
Sharon, Margalit Zimmerman
	("Gali") (first wife), 34, 40, 45
Sharon, Omri (daughter), 45, 91
Shehada, Salah, 24
Shlomzion Party, 56
Sinai Desert
	and Egyptian buildup, 48
	and peace between Egypt and
		Israel, 57-58, 59
	and Six-Day War, 42, 43
	and Suez War, 39
	and War of Attrition, 45-46
	and Yom Kippur War, 51
Six-Day War, 42-44, 46, 57
Solomon, King, 26
Soviet Union
	and Egyptian aid, 38, 46
	and Yom Kippur War, 53
Straits of Tiran, 42
Suez Canal
	and Egyptian buildup, 48-49
	and Six-Day War, 43
	and War of Attrition, 45-46
	and Yom Kippur War, 52, 53
Suez War, 38-39, 40
suicide bombers, 15-17, 19, 21,
	22, 24, 90, 92, 93
	women as, 21, 22, 23
Syria
	and Lebanese civil war, 60
	and Six-Day War, 42
	and war at creation of state of
		Israel, 32
	and Yom Kippur War, 50-53

Taqatqa, Andaleeb, 23
Tawalbe, Mahmoud, 22

Tel Aviv
   violence between Israelis and
      Palestinians in, 17, 19, 89, 93
   and war at creation of state of
      Israel, 32
television incident, and Sharon's
   re-election as prime minister,
   14-15
Temple Mount, Sharon's visit to, 84-87
Tenet, George, 93

United Nations
   and Palestine, 31
   and state of Israel, 31
   and Suez War, 39
   and 2000 intifada, 86-87
   and truce in war at creation of
      state of Israel, 33
   and Yom Kippur War, 52-53
United States
   and Israeli attack on Lebanon, 80
   and negotiations between Israel
      and Palestinians, 81-83, 84, 91-93
   and peace agreement between
      Israel and Egypt, 57-59
   and Sharon, 21, 90, 93
   and Yom Kippur War, 51, 52-53

War of Attrition, 45-46
West Bank
   fence separating Israel from
      settlements on, 24
   Israel closing main roads of, 24
   and Palestinian Authority, 15
   Palestinian control of, 78, 79, 83
   in Palestinian state, 21
   and safe passage for Palestinians,
      84
   Sharon building settlements on,
      56-57, 60, 80, 83, 88, 91-92
   and Six-Day War, 44
   and trenches around towns in,
      90
   violence between Israelis and
      Palestinians in, 17, 18-19, 22,
      81, 91, 92
Western Wall, 81
World War I, 28
World War II, 30, 31
Wye River Memorandum, 83

Yom Kippur War, 50-53, 55

Zeevi, Rehavam, 18
Zionism, 28

page:

2:   KRT/NMI
11: 21st Century Publishing
13: Zuma Press/NMI
16: KRT/NMI
20: KRT/NMI
27: New Millennium Images
30: © Bettmann/CORBIS
33: AP/Wide World Photos
36: AP/Wide World Photos
41: © Milner Moshe/CORBIS SYGMA
44: AFP/NMI
47: AP/Wide World Photos
50: AFP/NMI

55: AFP/NMI
59: AFP/NMI
62: AFP/NMI
64: AFP/NMI
67: © David Rubinger/CORBIS
71: AFP/NMI
74: KRT/NMI
77: AP/Wide World Photos
82: KRT/NMI
85: Reuters Photo Archive/NMI
86: KRT/NMI
89: AFP/NMI
92: AFP/NMI

Cover: AP/Wide World Photos
Frontis: KRT/NMI

RICHARD WORTH has thirty years' experience as a writer, trainer, and video producer. He has written more than 25 books, including *The Four Levers of Corporate Change*, a best-selling business book. Many of his books are for young adults on topics that include family living, foreign affairs, biography, history, and the criminal justice system.

ARTHUR M. SCHLESINGER, jr. is the leading American historian of our time. He won the Pulitzer Prize for his book *The Age of Jackson* (1945) and again for a chronicle of the Kennedy administration, *A Thousand Days* (1965), which also won the National Book Award. Professor Schlesinger is the Albert Schweitzer Professor of the Humanities at the City University of New York and has been involved in several other Chelsea House projects, including the series REVOLUTIONARY WAR LEADERS, COLONIAL LEADERS, and YOUR GOVERNMENT.